THE BOXER

This graphic novel is based on the book *Harry Haft: Auschwitz Survivor, Challenger of Rocky Marciano* by Alan Scott Haft, published by Syracuse University Press (2006)

SELF MADE HERO

First published in English 2014
by SelfMadeHero
139 -141 Pancras Road
London NW1 1UN
www.selfmadehero.com

Author and Artist: Reinhard Kleist
Cover design: Reinhard Kleist and Nebojsa Tabacki
Translated by: Michael Waaler

Based on the book:
Harry Haft: Auschwitz Survivor, Challenger of Rocky Marciano

GOETHE-INSTITUT

The translation of this work was supported by the Goethe-Institut which is funded by the German Ministry of Foreign Affairs

Publishing Assistant: Guillaume Rater
Editorial & Production Manager: Lizzie Kaye
Sales & Marketing Manager: Sam Humphrey
Publishing Director: Emma Hayley
With thanks to: Nick de Somogyi and Jane Laporte

A CIP record for this book is available from the British Library

ISBN: 978-1-906838-77-5

10 9 8 7 6 5 4 3 2 1

Printed and bound in China

Reinhard Kleist

THE BOXER

The true story of Holocaust Survivor Harry Haft

SELF MADE HERO

MIAMI, SEPTEMBER 1963.
SEASIDE TERRACE
MIAMI HOTEL APTS.
AIR CONDITION
N MIAMI AVE
1/4 MILE
MOTEL
CLICK
NO MUSIC!
WHEN DAD SPOKE, THERE WAS NO DISCUSSION.
I WOULD HAVE RATHER BEEN AT THE POOL WITH MY BROTHER AND SISTER...
...BUT DAD INSISTED I GO WITH HIM.

I WAS OFTEN SCARED OF HIM. TO ME, HE WAS THE TOUGHEST GUY IN THE WORLD. I MEAN, HE'D BEEN A BOXER!
HE WASN'T THE KIND OF DAD WHO PLAYED BASEBALL WITH HIS SON, AND HE WAS OFTEN HOT-TEMPERED.
MOM WOULD TRY AND MAKE UP FOR HIS OUTBURSTS BY TELLING ME ABOUT HIS TERRIFYING PAST.
I DIDN'T WANNA HEAR ABOUT IT.
THE NOW WAS BAD ENOUGH.

URGH...
IT'S GOOD YOU CAME TODAY.
ONE DAY, I'LL TELL YOU EVERYTHING.

1

BEŁCHATOW,
POLAND, 1939.

WHY IS IT ME WHO ALWAYS HAS TO GO OVER THE BORDER AND NEVER YOU TWO?
BECAUSE YOU'RE THE SMALLEST.
NOW STOP PROCRASTINATING, HERTZKO!
LEAVE HIM BE, ARIA. MEIR'S GIRL'S COMING WITH HIS GOODS.
HAVE YOU BEEN WAITING...?
MY BROTHER'S GOING WITH YOU. HE'S GOT THE CLOTH FROM MY DAD.
I'M SUPPOSED TO CROSS THE BORDER WITH THAT IDIOT?!
YOU GOT A PROBLEM WITH THAT?
HE'S RETARDED...
HE CAN RUN JUST AS WELL AS ANYONE ELSE.
OR ARE YOU SCARED OF HIM?
N...NO.
OK — HE CAN COME.

WE'VE GOT TO GET DOWN TO THE RIVER AND THEN KEEP HEADING EAST.
SURE THING, HERTZKO!
QUIET, YOU IDIOT, OR DO YOU WANT THE GERMANS TO CATCH US?
I WAS FOURTEEN YEARS OLD WHEN THE GERMANS MARCHED INTO BEŁCHATOW IN '39.

POLAND WAS SPLIT INTO THE OCCUPIED ZONE AND THE SO-CALLED GENERAL GOVERNMENT. THE BORDER RAN CLOSE TO WHERE WE LIVED.
THOSE PEOPLE WITH FAMILIES WITH GERMAN BACKGROUNDS WELCOMED THE OCCUPIERS. WE WATCHED TERRIFIED AS THEY MARCHED DOWN THE STREETS.
LIFE IN OUR SMALL TOWN CHANGED OVERNIGHT.
OGŁOSZENIE
ESPECIALLY FOR US JEWS.

WE HAFTS WERE ANYTHING BUT RICH.
MY FATHER SOLD FRUIT AND VEGETABLES AT THE MARKET AND HAD HIS HANDS FULL GETTING US BY. HE AND MOM MADE A STRANGE COUPLE. I WAS THE YOUNGEST OF EIGHT.
ONE DAY, DAD GOT SICK WITH TYPHUS. BEFORE HE DIED, HE CALLED ARIA, MY BROTHER, TO HIM.
ARIA, YOU HAVE TO BE A FATHER TO MY CHILDREN NOW...

SOON AFTER, MY FAMILY FELL APART. MY SISTERS WENT TO ŁODZ. ONLY ARIA, PERETZ AND I STAYED WITH OUR MOTHER.
EVERYONE HAD TO HELP. I WAS FIVE WHEN I GOT MY FIRST JOB, TAKING GEESE FROM THE MARKET FOR SLAUGHTER.
rzeźnik koszerny
I NEVER THOUGHT ABOUT THOSE POOR GEESE BEING KILLED. I JUST THOUGHT ABOUT THE WARM BREAD I COULD BUY US WITH THE MONEY.
AT SCHOOL, WE LEARNED THAT JEWS AND CHRISTIANS WEREN'T THE SAME.
WHICH OF YOU CAN TELL ME WHO THE LORD JESUS WAS MURDERED BY...?

HAFT!
I'LL TEACH YOU NOT TO SLEEP IN CLASS, YOU CUTTHROAT JEW!
I DIDN'T GO TO SCHOOL FOR AS LONG AS THE OTHER KIDS...
I WAS JUST TRYING TO...
YOU'RE A GOOD FOR NOTHING!
BUT I HAD TO PROMISE DAD TO KEEP YOU ON THE STRAIGHT AND NARROW...
PAF
DAMMIT!!!
NO, ARIA, STOP!!
FROM THEN ON, I HAD TO WORK ALL THE TIME OTHERWISE I GOT A BEATING.

THEY GOT iT WORSE ON THE OTHER SiDE THAN US. WE CAN SELL THEM FOOD. MEiR PABLANSKi AND HiS PEOPLE ARE COMiNG iN ON iT, TOO.
OY! THiS FAMiLY HAS ALREADY BEEN TORN APART AND NOW YOU WANT TO PUT US ALL iN DANGER?
TAKE A LOOK AROUND YOU, MOM. THERE'S NO WORK AND NO MONEY!
I'M iN!
ME TOO!
WE WERE NOW A PART OF THE GERMAN REiCH. THOSE POOR SWiNE UNDER THE GENERAL GOVERNMENT OF POLAND A FEW MiLES FARTHER EAST HAD iT EVEN WORSE. THANKS TO THE SMUGGLiNG, WE AT LEAST HAD SOMETHiNG TO EAT.
EVERYTHiNG WAS FORBiDDEN TO US JEWS. YOU COULD BE DRAGGED OFF TO FORCED LABOUR AT ANY MOMENT. WE WEREN'T ALLOWED TO TRAVEL, AND THERE WAS A CURFEW. EVENTUALLY THE GERMANS CRAMMED US iNTO A GHETTO.

THE BORDER MUST BE HERE.
HALT! DON'T MOVE!
RUN!!!
Bang
HERTZKO!

WHAT HAPPENED? WHY ARE YOU BACK ALREADY?!
WE RAN INTO A PATROL!
HE'S BLEEDING!
WHAT'S YOUR NAME?
I'M LEAH. LEAH PABLANSKI. YOUR BROTHER'S IN BUSINESS WITH MY FATHER.
YOU'RE BEAUTIFUL...
AND YOU'RE VERY BRAVE...
...AND ALSO A LITTLE STUPID.

ONE OF YOUR LOT MUST HAVE GIVEN AWAY THE ROUTE!
HOW STUPID DO YOU THINK WE ARE?! IT MUST HAVE BEEN ONE OF YOUR LOT!
WE'LL SEE ABOUT THAT!
ARIA!
WHO'S NEXT? HUH?!

WE AIN'T FINISHED, ARIA HAFT!
THEY'RE GONE. YOU CAN CALM DOWN!
DON'T EVEN THINK ABOUT GIVING ME A BEATING.
INCREDIBLE! YOU KNOCKED MEIR PABLANSKI ON HIS BACK!
NOT BAD, KID.
MEIR? OH NO...
DON'T SWEAT IT. HE'LL BE OK.
IT'S JUST... HE'S... HE'S LEAH'S DAD...
YOU GOT YOUR EYE ON THE GIRL, HUH? WELL, I GUESS YOU'RE JUST GONNA HAVE TO BITE THE BULLET! HAHA!
BUT THAT'S NOT A BAD HOOK YOU GOT THERE, LITTLE BROTHER!

YOU'VE GOT SOME CHUTZPAH SHOWING YOUR FACE HERE!
I BROUGHT A HAM. I WANTED TO SAY SORRY.
I CAN SAY GOODBYE TO MY TEETH. THE GERMANS HAVE CONFISCATED ALL OUR DOCTORS' EQUIPMENT.
I ALSO WANTED TO ASK IF I COULD TAKE OUT LEAH...?
AND WHY SHOULD I LET MY DAUGHTER GO OUT WITH A HOT-HEAD LIKE YOU?
I WAS JUST TRYING TO PROTECT MY FAMILY. SO, ARE YOU GONNA TAKE THE HAM OR NOT?
HE'S BROUGHT SOMETHING TO EAT.
OY! WHAT CAN I SAY TO THAT...?

LET'S GET MARRIED, LEAH. RIGHT NOW. THERE'S NO REASON TO WAIT. EVERYTHING'S CRAZY RIGHT NOW.
WE'LL TELL MY DAD FRIDAY EVENING...
...BUT IT WOULD BE BETTER IF YOU GOT YOUR BROTHER ARIA TO ARRANGE IT. DAD RESPECTS HIM.

Żydzi
zarejestrowany.
WHY DO THEY WANT US TO REGISTER OURSELVES?
PROBABLY FOR WORK DUTY. THANK GOD YOU'RE NOT SIXTEEN YET.
BUT I'LL HAVE TO DO IT. COME ON, LET'S GO HOME.
I NEED YOUR HELP, ARIA.
WHAT HAVE YOU DONE NOW?
I WANNA MARRY LEAH.
AND WHAT'S THAT GOT TO DO WITH ME?
YOU HAVE TO TALK TO MEIR AND SORT IT OUT WITH HIM.
HM...
WELL, I DON'T SEE ANY REASON TO WAIT. EVERYTHING'S GOING TO PIECES HERE ANYWAY...
MEIR'S A GOOD GUY. IF THAT'S WHAT YOU REALLY WANT, YOU GOT MY BLESSING.
I JUST DON'T GET WHY A GOOD-LOOKING GIRL FROM A GOOD FAMILY WANTS TO GET MIXED UP WITH A DOLT LIKE YOU...
I'LL TELL MOM. IT'LL CHEER HER UP.
I'M GOING TO REGISTER. I'LL BE BACK FOR LUNCH.

OY OY OY!
NOW YOU WANT TO LEAVE ME TOO?!
ROSA IS IN RUSSIA, RIFKA IN ŁODZ, AND BRANDEL'S NEVER AROUND SINCE SHE GOT MARRIED, TOO.
ACH! BUT I DON'T WANT TO STICK MY NOSE INTO YOUR AFFAIRS...
LEAH AND I LOVE EACH OTHER, MOM, AND WE'RE NOT GOING ANYWHERE...
AT LEAST I'VE STILL GOT ARIA.
NOW GO AND FIND YOUR BROTHER. IT'S ALMOST EVENING AND HE STILL ISN'T BACK FROM THAT STUPID REGISTRATION.
HEY! DID YOU REGISTER?!
ARE YOU MESHUGGAH?!
NO ONE WHO'S REGISTERING IS COMING BACK.

NAME?
ARiA? WHAT ARE YOU STiLL DOiNG HERE?!
PSSST! WE AiN'T ALLOWED TO LEAVE. THEY'VE GOT OUR NAMES. iF I LEAVE NOW, THEY'LL FiND ME. AND YOU TOO!
YOU'VE GOTTA GET OUT OF HERE!
THEY TOLD US THEY'RE PUTTiNG US ON WORK DETAiL TONiGHT. YOU'VE GOTTA TAKE OFF AND LOOK AFTER MOM.
PLEASE, ARiA. I'LL DiSTRACT THEM AND YOU MAKE A RUN FOR iT!

HICCUP!!
WHAT'S THE MEANING OF THIS? THAT JEW IS DRUNK!
WHO WAS THAT?! WHERE'S HE GOING?!
SOMEONE RAN OFF!
WHO WAS IT, JEW PIG?!
TALK!
Bang
CRACK

HOW SHOULD I KNOW?!?
CRACK
THAT'S ENOUGH. IF ONE OF THEM IS MISSING, WE'LL TAKE THIS ONE INSTEAD!
MOM...

JOZEF!
WITOLD!
ANNA!
GET BACK!
NO MATTER HOW HARD I LOOKED FOR MY FAMILY ALONG WITH EVERYONE ELSE, NONE OF THEM SHOWED.
NO ONE ON THE BUS KNEW WHERE THEY WERE TAKING US. AND AS THE LIGHTS OF BEŁCHATOW DISAPPEARED BEHIND THE HILLS, I REALIZED SOMETHING...
...FROM THAT MOMENT ON, I WAS ALONE.

I'D NEVER BEEN ALONE. MY FAMILY HAD ALWAYS BEEN THERE.
AND I'D NEVER REALLY BEEN OUT OF BEŁCHATOW.
THE LONELINESS FELL ON ME LIKE A WAVE.

WHAT HAPPENED TO YOUR HANDS, KID?
DON'T TOUCH ME!

I LEFT THE LIFE I'D KNOWN BEHIND IN THE NIGHT AND HELD ON TO ONE THOUGHT:
I HAD TO SEE LEAH AGAIN.
COLOMB
THE BUSES DROVE THROUGH TILL MORNING. WE PASSED POZNAN AND SOON WE REACHED A CAMP OUTSIDE THE CITY.

WE NEED VOLUNTEERS TO WORK WAREHOUSE DUTY. COME ON, SHOW YOUR HANDS!
MOST OF THE VOLUNTEERS WERE CRIMINALS AND THUGS LOOKING TO WIN FAVOUR BEING CRONIES.
LINE UP! FASTER, FASTER!
LEFT!
RIGHT!
LEFT!
LEFT!
RIGHT!

LEFT.
RIGHT.
I WAS SENT TO THE RIGHT. I NEVER SAW THE MEN SENT TO THE LEFT AGAIN.
LISTEN UP, I'M YOUR KAPO.
I'M RESPONSIBLE FOR MAKING SURE THAT THE RULES ARE OBEYED HERE. SO IF YOU DON'T WANT ANY TROUBLE, STICK TO THE GERMANS' RULES.
HEY, YOU THERE!
I KNEW THE KAPO. HE WAS A CROOK FROM BEŁCHATOW.
TOUCH ME AND I'LL BREAK EVERY BONE IN YOUR BODY!!!

MOM...
LEAH...
ONE
TWO
THREE
FOUR
FIVE
I WAS GIVEN CEMENT WORK.
THE FOREMAN WAS A CIVILIAN WHO WORKED FOR A CONSTRUCTION COMPANY.
FASTER! THIS ISN'T A VACATION!

I DIDN'T HAVE A MOMENT SPARE TO CURSE MY FATE.
MAKE SURE YOU DON'T SPILL ANY, OR YOU CAN GO WITHOUT RATIONS.
I FELL EXHAUSTED INTO MY BED EVERY EVENING. MORNINGS I WAS WOKEN BY THE SHOUTS OF THE KAPOS.
WHAT WAS I DOING HERE?
I HADN'T DONE ANYTHING TO THE GERMANS...
SET UP AN ENGINE HOUSE HERE!
DID I AT LEAST MANAGE TO GET ARIA OUT?
WHAT WAS GOD THINKING SENDING ME HERE INSTEAD OF HIM?
AFTER A COUPLE OF WEEKS I BEGAN WONDERING...
...WHAT THE HEAVILY GUARDED RAILROAD CARS THAT OFTEN STOOD ON THE PARALLEL TRACKS WERE HOLDING.

HEY, YOU! COME HERE!
WHAT HAPPENED TO YOUR HANDS?
BROKEN.
YOU'RE DAMN YOUNG TO BE HERE.
THERE WAS A MIX-UP.
PFFF... THESE ARE CRAZY TIMES! IT'S IMPOSSIBLE TO TELL A FRIEND FROM AN ENEMY ANYMORE.
THEY SENT MY BROTHER TO DACHAU FOR BEING A COMMUNIST. AND I'M BREAKING MY BACK HERE FOR THE "REICH". YOU HEARD OF DACHAU?
NO.
LUCKY YOU.
BIT BY BIT, I BEGAN BEFRIENDING THE FOREMAN.
SOON I TRUSTED HIM ENOUGH TO PLUCK UP THE COURAGE TO ASK HIM A QUESTION.
WHAT ARE THOSE CARS LOADED WITH ANYWAY?

SUPPLIES FOR TROOPS IN THE GENERAL GOVERNMENT. WHY YOU ASKING?
WELL, BECAUSE THEY'RE GUARDED LIKE THAT...
...CURIOUS, HUH? I'VE ALWAYS WONDERED MYSELF WHAT LUXURIES THEY'RE SPOILING FOLKS BACK THERE WITH.
GET BACK TO WORK!
WHY DID HE WINK AT ME LIKE THAT? DID IT MEAN HE'D LET ME GET CLOSE TO THE CARS? AND IF SO, COULD I HIDE IN ONE OF THEM AND ESCAPE? BACK TO BEŁCHATOW, TO LEAH?

THE NEXT MORNING, THE FOREMAN ACTUALLY LET ME APPROACH THE GOODS CARS WITHOUT TROUBLE.
HEY, PSST!
WHAT DO YOU THINK OF THESE? CIGARS! I COULD HAVE GOTTEN MORE.
NOT BAD, KID. WHAT'S YOUR NAME?
HERTZKO.
I'M KARELLER. COME HERE.
THE GUARDS LET KARELLER'S CAR PASS THROUGH THE GATES NO PROBLEM AND HE HEADED TOWARDS POZNAN.

RINI DARLING! LOOK WHAT I'VE GOT!
GIVE THE KID SOMETHING TO EAT.
AND? YOU GOT A GIRL?
♪

IT TURNED OUT THAT KARELLER HAD THREE MORE GIRLS AROUND POZNAN...
...BUT I LIKED RINI THE BEST.
YEAH, AT HOME IN BEŁCHATOW. I COULDN'T EVEN SAY GOODBYE WHEN THEY TOOK ME AWAY.
WRITE HER A LETTER IF YOU LIKE.
JEWS AREN'T ALLOWED TO SEND MAIL...
DOES SHE HAVE FRIENDS WHO AREN'T JEWISH?
YEAH, ZOSCHA KUBIAK. I KNOW THE ADDRESS!
BUT... BUT THERE'S SOMETHING ELSE.
THERE IS SOMETHING...
IT'S... I... I CAN'T WRITE...
THEN TELL ME WHAT I SHOULD WRITE TO HER.
PLEASE WRITE THAT I'M OK AND THAT I'LL BE FINE.
...AND THAT YOU'RE ONLY THINKING ABOUT HER.
YEAH, THAT TOO! YOU KNOW JUST WHAT TO WRITE, HUH?!
YEAH, WOMEN KNOW THESE THINGS.
AND LIFE IN THE CAMP IS TERRIBLE. THE WORK IS HARD AND THE FOOD IS DISGUSTING. THE KAPOS ARE GANGSTERS. I KNOW A FEW FROM BEŁCHATOW. BUT THANK GOD I'VE GOT THE FOREMAN ON MY SIDE. HE'S HELPING ME. THAT'S HOW I CAN SEND YOU THIS LETTER. YOU AND MY FAMILY ARE ALWAYS IN MY THOUGHTS. THAT'S HOW I SURVIVE THESE DIFFICULT TIMES.
YOUR HERTZKO

BEŁCHATOW, 1941
MY DEAR HERTZKO!
I'M SO HAPPY THAT YOU'RE OK. THE SITUATION HERE IN THE GHETTO KEEPS GETTING WORSE. MY FATHER IS SICK WITH TYPHUS. I'M NOT SURE WHAT WILL HAPPEN! YOUR BROTHER ARIA HELPS US WITH FOOD. THERE IS NONE TO BE FOUND ELSEWHERE. OH, IF ONLY I COULD LEAVE THIS TERRIBLE COUNTRY AND GO TO AMERICA WITH YOU AT MY SIDE.
YOUR LOVING
LEAH
AS LONG AS I KEPT KARELLER IN GOODS, I COULD KEEP VISITING RINI AND GET MY MAIL.
A LETTER FROM MY FAMILY!! PLEASE READ IT, RINI!
YOUR BROTHER WRITES THAT HE'S STILL SMUGGLING AND THAT THEY'RE GETTING BY JUST FINE.
AND HE'S HELPING OTHERS!
WHAT STUFF DOES YOUR BROTHER SMUGGLE THEN?
ANYTHING YOU CAN THINK OF!
ASK HIM IF HE CAN GET HOLD OF DOLLARS OR GOLD.
HE CAN GET HOLD OF ANYTHING. WE JUST HAVE TO TELL HIM.
BUT NOT BY MAIL. WE'LL DRIVE.
KARELLER ARRANGED FOR IT THAT I COULD ACCOMPANY HIM TO BEŁCHATOW. I'D GET TO SEE EVERYONE AGAIN. MY FAMILY. LEAH! MY HEART WAS BEATING LIKE CRAZY.

OH MY GOD! WHAT HAPPENED?
LEAH!!!
AND WHERE'S YOUR BROTHER?
WE SHOULD HEAD OVER TO MY SISTER, BRANDEL. SHE'LL KNOW WHERE EVERYONE IS!
EVERYONE ON! MOVE IT! NOW!

MY BABY!
HERE! CATCH!
AAAH!!!
Bang
HA HA
HA
BRANDEL!
IT'S TOO DANGEROUS HERE. WE HAVE TO LEAVE!
NOT A WORD ABOUT THIS WHEN WE GET BACK.

MY SISTER... HER WITH THE BABY... AND ME? I DIDN'T DO A THING...
WHAT COULD YOU HAVE DONE, HUH?!
I'D LOST ALL HOPE OF SEEING ANY OF MY FAMILY ALIVE AGAIN.
THERE WAS NO GOD FOR ME ANYMORE.
WOULD YOU LIKE ME TO WRITE A LETTER FOR YOU?
NO.

A FEW MONTHS LATER, WE WERE WOKEN IN THE MIDDLE OF THE NIGHT AND FORCED INTO CATTLE CARS.
THE JOURNEY FELT LIKE A WEEK. NO FOOD, NOTHING TO DRINK. THE AIR STANK OF OUR FAECES.
AT THE END, ALL WE HEARD WERE THE SIGHS OF THE DYING BENEATH OUR FEET.
THERE WAS NO GOD.

EVERYONE OUT!
MOVE iT!
PANG
HEY, WHAT'S YOUR NAME?
SCHLEMEK PODROWSKi.
LiSTEN TO ME, SCHLEMEK. WE WATCH OUT FOR EACH OTHER AND SOMEHOW WE'LL GET THROUGH THIS.
DEAL. WHAT'S YOUR NAME?
HERTZKO... HERTZKO HAFT.
I STAYED FOR A MONTH iN STRZELiN.

GET UP!
BANG
WOULD YOU HELP ME IF I COULDN'T GO ON LIKE THAT GUY THERE?
SURE, WE STICK TOGETHER, RIGHT?
LIKE BROTHERS. I CAN'T IMAGINE A WORSE PLACE ON EARTH THAN THIS.
HOW WRONG I WAS.
ONE MORNING, WE DIDN'T GO TO WORK AS USUAL, BUT BACK INTO THE CATTLE CARS.
WHERE ARE YOU TAKING US?
TO YOUR GRAVES, JEW!
DON'T LISTEN TO HIM. THEY NEED PEOPLE TO WORK.
CLEAR TO GO!

TO THE LEFT!
TO THE RIGHT!
TO THE RIGHT!
TO THE LEFT!
WHERE HAD WE LANDED?
WAS THIS HELL?
44738
WHY DIDN'T THEY SEND US TO THE LEFT, TOO? WE WOULD HAVE GOTTEN BREAD, WATER, AND A SHOWER... I'M THIRSTY, TOO.
DON'T THINK ABOUT IT. AS LONG AS WE STICK TOGETHER, WE'LL GET OUT OF HERE SOMEHOW.
WATCH HOW I DO IT.
THAT NIGHT, SCHLEMEK AND I WERE ASSIGNED TO A WORK GROUP.

WE WERE LED TO THE BUILDING WITH THE CHIMNEY THAT DARKENED THE SKY.
I REGRETTED BEING ALIVE.
AND EVERY DAY THE HORRORS BECAME MORE UNBEARABLE.

GET A GRIP, HERTZKO, THEY'LL SHOOT YOU!
I CAN'T DO IT ANYMORE.
WHAT'S GOING ON? I'LL GET YOU MOVING!!!
I CAN'T DO IT...!

HERTZKO! DO WHAT HE SAYS!
BACK TO WORK!
LEAVE HIM!
I CAN USE HIM.

YOU OWE ME, JEW.
I'LL GET YOU ASSIGNED TO CANADA COMMANDO.
MAYBE IT WAS CALLED THAT BECAUSE CANADA IS A WEALTHY COUNTRY. I DON'T KNOW. WHATEVER THE CASE, I HAD TO SEARCH THROUGH THE CLOTHES OF THOSE DEPORTED FOR GOLD AND JEWELS.
THAT WAS FINE BY ME.
I'LL DO ANYTHING YOU WANT.
I'M SURE YOU WILL. CAN YOU KEEP A SECRET?
LOOK AT MY HANDS. I DIDN'T SAY A WORD WHEN YOUR PEOPLE WERE BREAKING THEM.
I'LL GET YOU THROUGH THIS ALIVE.
BUT YOU HAVE TO DO ME A FAVOUR.
BRING ME THE BOTTLE BACK ONCE YOU'VE FILLED IT.

A GUY FLIPPED OUT TODAY AT THE OVENS. HE FOUND HIS WIFE IN THE PILE...
I DON'T WANT TO HEAR ABOUT IT...
WHAT ABOUT YOU? YOU KNOW WHAT THEY'RE CALLING YOU NOW?
THE FAT JEW!
SO WHAT? I DON'T CARE.
DIDN'T YOU SAY THAT WE GOTTA STICK TOGETHER? AREN'T WE LIKE BLOOD BROTHERS? AND NOW YOU'RE SCHNEIDER'S DOG.
I'VE GOT HIM TO THANK FOR MY LIFE.
SO YOU DO ANYTHING THAT PIG TELLS YOU?
NOT EVERYTHING.
THOSE ARE THE CLOTHES OF THE PEOPLE I BURN THAT YOU SEARCH THROUGH FOR VALUABLES.
I DO IT FOR YOU, TOO... HERE.
NOW LET ME SLEEP.

SOON I'D COLLECTED ENOUGH JEWELS TO FILL THE BOTTLE AND GIVE IT BACK TO SCHNEIDER.
OUT, JEW!
WHAT'S THIS, HUH?
WHO ARE YOU SMUGGLING THE STONES OUT FOR?
TALK, PIG!
ENOUGH! TAKE HIM TO THE TRUCK.
I NEED HIM.
ON THE WAY OUT OF THE CAMP, I FELT SCHNEIDER GIVING ME A NEW BOTTLE.
IT WAS FULL OF WHISKY. I DRANK HALF OF IT.
...ANYONE WANNA SWAP A SWIG FOR A PIECE OF BREAD?
WITH EVERY YARD THAT THE TRUCK TOOK ME FROM AUSCHWITZ, I GAINED NEW COURAGE.
I NEVER SAW SCHLEMEK AGAIN.

AN HOUR LATER, THE TRUCK PASSED THROUGH THE GATES OF JAWORZNO COAL WORKS. I WAS PUT ON NIGHT SHIFT IN THE SHAFTS.
HEY, MISCHA.
MISCHA, IT'S ME, HERTZKO FROM BEŁCHATOW...
WHY ARE YOU HELPING THESE PIGS?
SHUT YOUR MOUTH! I DON'T KNOW YOU!
NOW GET UP!
MOVE!
LEFT, RIGHT, LEFT...
WE WORKED SIX DAYS A WEEK IN THE MINES.
I LOST ALL SENSE OF TIME.
MISCHA SEEMED TO ENJOY BEATING ME IN FRONT OF THE GUARDS.

THAT'S ENOUGH!
DID I DREAM IT?
AT THAT MOMENT, SCHNEIDER SEEMED LIKE A GOD TO ME.
...I KNEW YOU'D STILL BE ALIVE.
HERE, TAKE THIS.
I UNDERSTOOD. FOR SCHNEIDER, SURVIVING WAS A DISTINCTION.
THANKS.
YOU'RE SOMEONE WHO ALWAYS GETS BACK UP ON HIS FEET.
FIRST WE STOLE A FEW DIAMONDS AND NOW WE MEET AT THIS LOUSY MINE.
HOW LIFE GOES...
I WANT TO SHOW YOU SOMETHING.
YOU SEE THAT? I'VE GOT A TATTOO, TOO. IT IDENTIFIES ME AS A MEMBER OF THE SS...
...IT EVEN SAYS MY BLOOD TYPE.
THE WAR'S NOT GOING WELL FOR US. WHEN IT'S OVER, I'LL HAVE TO PAY FOR ALL THIS HERE.

AND WHAT'S THAT GOT TO DO WITH ME?
IF I HELP YOU SURVIVE, YOU'LL BE IN MY DEBT. I WANT YOU TO TELL THEM THAT I'M NOT LIKE THE OTHERS. WOULD YOU DO THAT?
YEAH... OF COURSE...
THANKS TO SCHNEIDER'S PROTECTION, I WAS GIVEN EASIER WORK AND REGULAR FOOD...
...WHICH I OFTEN TRADED FOR FAVOURS WITH THE FOREMAN.
WORD SLOWLY GOT AROUND THAT I WAS PROTECTED. MISCHA LEFT ME IN PEACE, AND THANKS TO THE FOOD FROM SCHNEIDER, I COULD EVEN PUT ON SOME WEIGHT.
HERTZKO! A NEW BATCH OF WORKERS HAS COME IN. I HEARD THAT YOUR BROTHER PERETZ IS ONE OF THEM.
WHERE?
I HEARD BLOCK 5.
PERETZ! PERETZ! HAFT!

PERETZ HAFT!
YES, SIR!
PERETZ, IT'S ME, HERTZKO! DON'T YOU RECOGNIZE ME?
LISTEN, I'M PROTECTED BY A GERMAN. I'LL EXPLAIN LATER. AND WATCH OUT FOR MISCHA!
HERE, I'VE STILL GOT SOME BREAD!
THAT CROOK IS HERE? THEY GOT HIM TOO, HUH?
HE'S WORSE THAN THE GERMANS...
SOMETIMES WE HAD TO STAND FOR HOURS AT ROLL CALL. ANYONE WHO FELL WAS TAKEN TO THE HOSPITAL AND NEVER SEEN AGAIN.
SCHNEIDER ARRANGED AT MY REQUEST FOR MY BROTHER TO BE GIVEN EASIER WORK CLOSE TO ME.

DON'T GIVE UP!
AND MISCHA LEFT US IN PEACE.
I PRAY TO GOD THAT MOM, RIFKA AND BRANDEL ARE OK.
GOD? LOOK AROUND YOU. IF THERE WAS A GOD, WOULD HE LET THIS HAPPEN?
BARUCH ATA ADONAI...
LEAH... HOW I MISSED HER.
I'D HAVE GIVEN MY LIFE TO FEEL HER HAND ON MINE JUST ONCE.

WALK WITH ME. LET'S TALK.
I'VE GOT NEW PLANS FOR YOU.
YOU'VE GOTTEN STRONG, LITTLE JEW. I'LL TURN YOU INTO AN ATTRACTION.
HOW?
I'LL MAKE YOU A BOXER. YOU'LL HELP THE OFFICERS AND SOLDIERS HERE IN THE CAMP PASS THE TIME. WHAT DO YOU SAY?
I'LL DO ANYTHING YOU SAY.
THAT'S WHAT I THOUGHT. THAT'S WHY I CHOSE YOU.
THE FIGHT WILL TAKE PLACE IN FRONT OF THE OFFICERS' QUARTERS. THE FIGHT'S FINISHED WHEN ONE OF YOU CAN'T FIGHT ANY LONGER. IT'S THAT SIMPLE.
WHO AM I UP AGAINST? ONE OF THE GUARDS?
A VOLUNTEER. HE RECEIVES SPECIAL RATIONS.
I'VE NEVER REALLY BOXED BEFORE.
I'LL TEACH YOU SOME TECHNIQUES. SOME OF THE STUFF YOU LEARN IN THE SS.
THE FIGHT IS NEXT SUNDAY!

CURVE IN YOUR LEFT WHEN YOU PUNCH.
YOU SEE? IT GIVES YOU MOMENTUM!
TELL ME, IF YOU KNOW THAT YOU'LL HAVE TO PAY FOR ALL THIS, WHY DO IT?
IF YOU'D HAD A CHOICE LIKE ME, WHICH SIDE WOULD YOU HAVE CHOSEN? THE WOLVES OR THE SHEEP?
I DIDN'T HAVE A CHOICE.
BUT NOW... SHOW THEM WHAT YOU CAN DO!
AND WHEN IT'S ALL OVER? WHAT WILL I BE FOR YOU THEN? A WOLF... OR A SHEEP?
YOU'RE NOT DUMB, KID. YOU'RE A TOUGH GUY, NOT LIKE THE OTHERS. YOU CAN BE PROUD OF THAT.
BUT IF YOU WANT TO SURVIVE HERE, LEARN SOME GERMAN. ADAPT.
IF YOU WANT TO HOWL WITH THE WOLVES, THEN SPEAK THEIR LANGUAGE.
ASK ME IF THERE'S SOMETHING YOU WANT TO KNOW...
HERE. YOU CAN WEAR MY OLD WINTER GLOVES TO PROTECT YOUR BONES.

HERE COMES YOUR FIRST OPPONENT!
THE MAN HADN'T VOLUNTEERED.
NOW I KNEW WHAT WAS MEANT BY...
..."WHEN ONE OF YOU CAN'T FIGHT ANY LONGER."

I WAS SURE THEY'D SHOOT ME iF I REFUSED.
FiNiSH HiM!

HAHA!
YES! I HAD MONEY ON THE LITTLE ONE!
THE WINNER... IN THE RIGHT CORNER!
WHAT HAPPENS TO HIM?
DON'T WORRY ABOUT IT.
YOU'RE STILL IN THE RING. THAT'S ALL THAT COUNTS.
HE WOULD HAVE ENDED UP IN AUSCHWITZ SOONER OR LATER ANYWAY.
THE ENTERTAINMENT PROGRAM BECAME A WEEKLY EVENT.

EVERY SUNDAY, I HAD TO FIGHT SIX HALF-DEAD OPPONENTS.
I SOON LEARNED HOW TO KEEP THE PUBLIC INTERESTED BY PLAYING CAT AND MOUSE WITH MY OPPONENTS.
I NEVER THOUGHT ABOUT THE MEN BEING KILLED, ONLY ABOUT SURVIVING.
I QUICKLY EARNED MY NICKNAME:
HERE COMES THE JEWISH BEAST!

LISTEN... THERE'S ONLY ONE FIGHT TODAY, BUT THE STAKES ARE HIGH.
A COUPLE OF GENERALS ARE COMING FROM BERLIN. THEY'VE PUT MONEY ON HAVING A WORTHY CHALLENGER FOR YOU. WE'VE ALL BET AGAINST THEM.
SO DON'T LET US DOWN, HERTZKO!
YOU PUT MONEY ON ME?
YEP. AND NOT A SMALL AMOUNT. SO, IF YOU LOSE, THERE'S NOT A GUARD HERE WHO'LL BE TOO HAPPY WITH YOU.
DON'T WORRY. I WON'T LOSE.
THEY SAY HE STANDS UNBEATEN. BUT I'VE WAGERED, TOO.
AND FORGET THE GLOVES. YOUR CHALLENGER WON'T BE USING ANY EITHER.
AND IF I LOSE... WHAT THEN?
IT WAS ONLY THEN THAT I REALIZED THAT SCHNEIDER HAD CALLED ME BY NAME.

BARK
IN THE RIGHT CORNER.. THE JEWISH BEAST OF JAWORZNO!
IN THE OTHER CORNER.. THE FRENCH HEAVYWEIGHT CHAMPION OF '34!

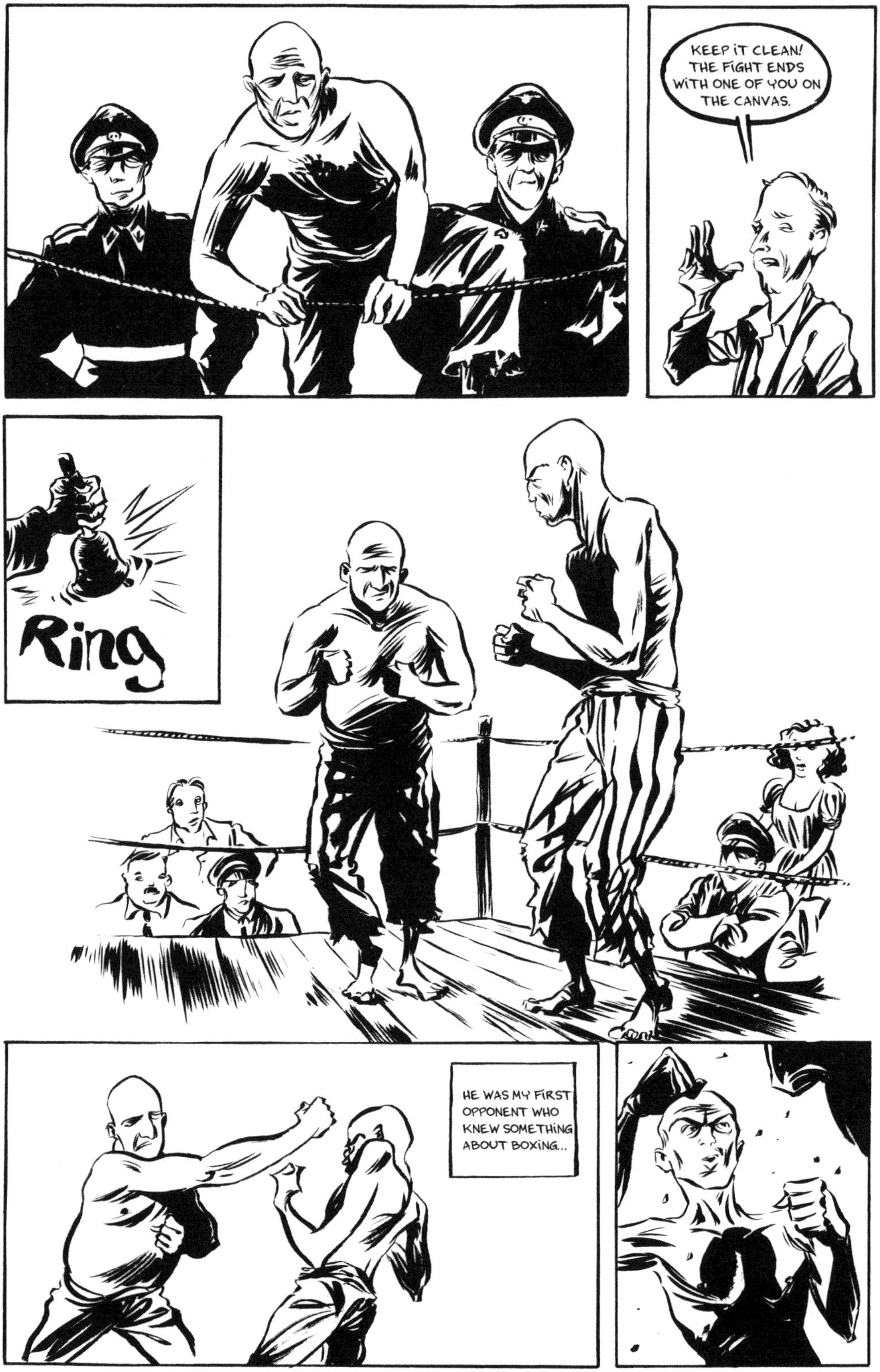
KEEP iT CLEAN! THE FiGHT ENDS WiTH ONE OF YOU ON THE CANVAS.
Ring
HE WAS MY FiRST OPPONENT WHO KNEW SOMETHiNG ABOUT BOXiNG...

HiT HiM!
COME ON!
FiNiSH HiM!
BaRK
AFTER FOUR OR FiVE ROUNDS, I WAS BLEEDiNG BADLY FROM DEEP CUTS AROUND THE EYES. I COULD HARDLY SEE ANYTHiNG.
BUT iN THE SEVENTH, THE FRENCHMAN MADE A MiSTAKE...

BARK
THE WINNER!!!

Bang
I NEVER HEARD ANYTHING ABOUT THE FRENCHMAN AGAIN.
NOW I EVEN HAD A NAME OVER THE BORDER. I THOUGHT NOTHING COULD TOUCH ME...
...SO LONG AS I STAYED CLOSE TO SCHNEIDER.

IS IT THE RUSSIANS?
BOOM
BOOM
THE DISTANT SOUND OF FIGHTING BECAME MORE AND MORE COMMON. IT SEEMED TO GET LOUDER EVERY NIGHT.
THEY'RE GETTING CLOSER...
THE GUARDS ARE GETTING WORRIED!
EVERYONE OUT!
MOVE IT!
BOOM
BOOM
MOVE OUT!
NOT LONG TILL WE'RE FREE!
THOSE TWO ARE MY PERSONAL SERVANTS. MAKE SURE THAT NOTHING HAPPENS TO THEM.
NIUUUUUUW
YESSIR!
NIUUUUUUW
PERETZ! LET'S GET IN THE FIRST ROW. IT'S SAFER THERE.

DRIVE. THERE'S NOTHING MORE TO DO HERE.
WHY DON'T THEY JUST LET US SNUFF IT IN THE CAMP?

WE MARCHED FOR DAYS.
OF THE THOUSANDS DRIVEN OUT ONTO THE STREET IN JAWORZNO, ONLY A FEW HUNDRED REACHED THE DESTINATION.
Bang
I WAS TOO WEAK TO COUNT THE DAYS WE SPENT IN THE WAGON. AROUND ME, I HEARD PEOPLE GROANING, CRYING, AND THEN...
...NOTHING.

WHEN THE DOORS OPENED AGAIN, ONLY A FEW OF US WERE STILL ALIVE.
HEY, YOU! WHERE ARE WE?
IT MUST BE FLOSSENBÜRG.

PERETZ, IN THERE...
WHY ARE THEY LOOKING AT US LIKE THAT?
WE'RE NEW. THAT MEANS LESS TO EAT.
LOOK. I KEPT SOME BREAD.
MAKE SURE NO ONE SEES IT.

THERE'S NOT GOING TO BE ANY MORE OF THAT FOR A LONG TIME.
WHY DO YOU SAY THAT?
THERE'S NO WORK HERE. THAT MEANS THERE'S NO REASON TO KEEP US ALIVE.
MAYBE SCHNEIDER WILL HELP US. HE'S HELPED US PLENTY IN THE PAST.
MMM... THAT'S GOOD.
PERETZ... SCHNEIDER CAN'T HELP US ANYMORE. HE DOESN'T EVEN KNOW WHERE WE ARE.
SO, WE'RE JUST GONNA DIE HERE LIKE EVERYONE ELSE?
DON'T GIVE UP. WE'VE SURVIVED EVERYTHING THEY'VE THROWN AT US SO FAR.
HOW CAN YOU BE SO CONFIDENT? WE'RE IN HELL!
THE BEST THING TO DO IS LIE STILL AND BE QUIET. WE HAVE TO KEEP OUR STRENGTH.

HERTZKO, WAKE UP!
DON'T MOVE!
WHAT'S WRONG?
LOOK!
OH MY GOD!

BROOOOOOOOOOOOO...
BOOM
WE WERE MOVED AGAIN. ANOTHER TRIP INTO THE UNKNOWN. BUT THE ALLIES WERE GETTING CLOSER AND OUR HOPES ROSE.
WE WERE TAKEN TO GROSS-ROSEN CONCENTRATION CAMP, WHERE WE EVEN GOT A LITTLE SOUP.
I USED EVERY MOMENT I THOUGHT I WASN'T BEING WATCHED TO STEAL SOMETHING I COULD TRADE FOR FOOD.
FROM THERE, WE WERE TAKEN TO AMBERG TO WORK IN A PLANE FACTORY, UNTIL THE BOMBS FELL THERE, TOO.
BUT INSTEAD OF JUST LEAVING US TO OUR FATE, WE WERE MOVED OUT AGAIN.

IT'S GOTTA BE CLOSE NOW?!
HERTZKO, WE'RE MOVING AWAY FROM THE FRONT!
IF WE DON'T RUN FOR iT NOW, PERETZ, WE'RE DEAD.
THEY'LL SHOOT US ON SiGHT!

Bang
THEY'RE GONNA SHOOT US ANYWAY!
HOW DO YOU KNOW THAT? YOU SAID IT YOURSELF, THEY ALWAYS NEED PEOPLE TO WORK.
WELL, I'M GOING.
I'M WITH YOU.
FOR THE LAST TIME, PERETZ! UP THERE, BY THE TREES. THAT'S OUR CHANCE!
NOT WITH ME!
JUST GIVE ME THE WORD.

NOW!
Bang
Bang

THERE THEY ARE!
LEAVE 'EM. THEY'RE LONG DEAD. DON'T WASTE THE BULLETS.

I WAS FREE... AFTER FOUR ENDLESS YEARS.
BUT I COULDN'T THINK OF ANYONE BUT MY BROTHER... MY MOM AND...
LEAH!!

THERE WAS NO JOY.
ONLY RAGE.
AND LONELINESS.

MMH.
AAAAH!!!
AAH!!!
AAH!!
AAH!!
AAH!

THE HUNGER ATE
INTO MY GUTS...

BANG
!
BANG
BANG

HELLO! CAN YOU HELP ME? I'M HURT.

PLEASE COME iN!
OF COURSE WE'LL HELP YOU, OFFiCER.
PLEASE EAT. YOU'RE STARViNG!
YOU CAN REST UPSTAiRS. MY WiFE WiLL BRiNG YOU FRESH TOWELS.

GOOD MORNING, SIR. YOU SLEPT A LONG TIME.
GOOD MORNING!
PLEASE, TELL US, WHICH ARMY GROUP ARE YOU WITH?
ERM... SOUTH.
AND WHAT HAPPENED TO YOUR EYE?
AN EXPLOSION...
LAST NIGHT YOU SLEPT WITHOUT THE EYE PATCH AND I COULDN'T SEE ANY INJURY... AND YOUR ACCENT... IT'S POLISH...
I...
WELL? EXPLAIN YOURSELF!

BANG
AAAAH!!!
BANG
BANG

44738

FREEZE!
HE'S SS!!

I SPEAK A LITTLE YIDDISH. WHAT'S YOUR NAME?
MY NAME IS HERTZKO HAFT. I'M FROM POLAND.
I ESCAPED FROM A CAMP.
WE'RE AMERICANS. I'M GREENBERG. I'M JEWISH, TOO. HAVE A CIGARETTE.
IS THE WAR OVER?
YOU HAVEN'T HEARD? WHERE'VE YOU BEEN THE WHOLE TIME?
IN THE FOREST.
TAKE OFF THAT UNIFORM. HERE ARE SOME NEW CLOTHES. WE'LL TAKE YOU TO STRAUBING.

BEKANNT-
MACHUNG

ARMY
THIS WAY, HERTZKO.

TODAY YOU GET A NEW PLACE TO LIVE.
WAIT IN THE CAR!
SHE'S THE WIFE OF SOME SS BIG SHOT. HE'S IN JAIL NOW.
AND NOW IT'S YOUR HOUSE.

AN HONEST-TO-GOD VILLA.
I WONDER IF IT HAD BELONGED TO JEWS FIRST?
LISTEN. WE NEED YOUR HELP.
THE ARMY FORBIDS US FROM FRATERNIZING WITH THE ENEMY.
I DON'T UNDERSTAND. WHAT DO YOU WANT ME TO DO ABOUT IT?
WOMEN!
HAHA!
YOU WANT ME TO GET YOU WOMEN!
IT DIDN'T TAKE LONG FOR WORD ABOUT OUR PLACE TO GET OUT OF TOWN.

G.I.S CAME FROM ALL OVER TO ENJOY A WILD NIGHT.
AND I WAS THEIR HOST.
HERTZKO, THERE'S SOMEONE AT THE DOOR LOOKING FOR YOU.
PERETZ!
AS HE LIVES AND BREATHES!
HERTZKO! I SAW YOU IN A PHOTO A G.I. WAS SHOWING AROUND. I JUST HAD TO COME HERE!
AND WHERE ARE YOU COMING FROM?
I SURVIVED THE DEATH MARCH AND WAS FREED BY THE AMERICANS. AND YOU? IS THIS YOUR PLACE?

COME IN, BROTHER!
PERETZ, BE MY PARTNER! WE'VE GOT EVERYTHING YOU COULD WISH FOR HERE: MONEY, WOMEN, SCHNAPPS!
IT'S A DARN SIGHT BETTER THAN LUGGING COAL FOR THE GERMANS!
I'M GOING TO GO BACK TO BEŁCHATOW.
YOU WANNA FIND LEAH, HUH?
THEN GO. I'LL KEEP THINGS RUNNING SMOOTHLY HERE TILL YOU GET BACK.

Belchatow
THE TRIP TOOK FOUR DAYS. THE TRAINS AND BUSES WERE FULL TO BURSTING WITH REFUGEES RETURNING TO POLAND. I DECIDED TO PAY A VISIT TO LEAH'S FRIEND ZOSCHA.
ZOSCHA! OPEN UP. IT'S ME, HERTZKO!
HERTZKO! OH MY GOD... YOU'RE ALIVE!
ZOSCHA, MY FAMILY... WHERE ARE THEY ALL?
COME IN.
ONE DAY THEY WERE PICKED UP, YOUR MOTHER AND BRANDEL AND RIFKA. I HEARD THEY WERE TAKEN TO TREBLINKA.
AND?
NO ONE CAME BACK.
AND ARIA?
HE JOINED THE RESISTANCE. SOMEONE TOLD ME HE WAS KILLED IN A SKIRMISH IN THE FOREST.
AND... HAVE YOU HEARD ANY NEWS OF LEAH?

IS SHE OK?
TELL ME SHE'S OK!
SHE MANAGED TO ESCAPE, BUT I DON'T KNOW IF SHE'S STILL ALIVE. I JUST KNOW SHE WASN'T DEPORTED.
THAT'S GOOD NEWS! WHERE DID SHE GO?
I DON'T KNOW. I'VE HAD NO SIGN OF LIFE FROM HER SINCE SHE LEFT.
PERETZ FOUND ME. I'M GOING TO FIND HER.
ALL TRACES OF THE OLD LIFE SEEMED TO HAVE BEEN OBLITERATED FROM THE CITY. THERE WERE HARDLY ANY JEWS TO BE SEEN IN THE STREETS.
I DIDN'T BELONG HERE ANYMORE.

MISCHA!
HEY!
HERTZKO, HOW GOOD TO SEE YOU...
SURPRISED TO SEE ME, HUH?!
STOP!
I... I WAS JUST TRYING TO SURVIVE!!!

I THOUGHT THEY'D SPARE ME IF I ACTED LIKE THEM...
AND WHAT ABOUT YOUR OWN PEOPLE, HUH?
THE ONLY THING THAT MATTERED WAS STAYING ALIVE. YOU KNOW THAT AS WELL AS ME! WHO WAS THE BEAST OF JAWORZNO, HUH?!!
WHO DO YOU THINK YOU'RE TALKING TO?!
HERTZKO, PLEASE DON'T!
DON'T KILL ME!!
NOT HERE... NOT AFTER EVERYTHING...

AND? HOW'S IT FEEL, HUH?
CLICK
NO! PLEASE!!
CLICK
CLICK
CLICK
NEXT TIME YOU WON'T BE SO LUCKY!
DAMMIT!
CLACK CLACK
BANG

WHEN I GOT BACK TO STRAUBING, I FOUND THE BORDELLO CLOSED.
I HAD TO TELL PERETZ ABOUT THE FATE OF OUR FAMILY.
THEY'RE ALL DEAD?
MOM... ARIA...
LIFE GOES ON, BROTHER... THAT'S SOMETHING I LEARNED ON MY TRIP.
...YEAH, WE'VE GOT TO KEEP GOING. WE OWE THEM THAT.
THAT'S WHY WE SURVIVED, RIGHT?
SO, WHAT'S OUR NEXT STEP?
WE NEED MONEY. SERGEANT DICKEY OFFERED ME SOME ACTION SMUGGLING CIGARETTES. IT'S A PROFITABLE BUSINESS.
LIKE BACK IN BEŁCHATOW, YOU KNOW?
AND WHAT'S THE BETTING I GET TO PLAY THE MULE?
NO ONE DOES IT BETTER THAN YOU, BROTHER!

MY JOB WAS TO DRIVE TO BERLIN AND SELL CRATES OF CIGARETTES STOLEN FROM FREIGHT CARS HERE.
BACK IN STRAUBING, I HAD A SUITCASE WITH A MILLION REICHSMARK IN IT.
HALT! HANDS IN THE AIR!
DON'T MOVE!!!

SOMEONE HAD SOLD US OUT.
PERETZ SPENT A COUPLE OF WEEKS IN JAIL. I COULDN'T GO BACK TO STRAUBING. I WAS A WANTED CRIMINAL THERE.
I FOUND SHELTER IN A REFUGEE CAMP ON THE AUSTRIAN-CZECH BORDER.
I DIDN'T DARE USE MY REAL NAME, SO I TOOK AN AUSTRIAN JEW UP ON HIS OFFER TO SELL ME HIS PAPERS FOR 500 DOLLARS. AT LEAST I STILL HAD ENOUGH MONEY FROM THE SMUGGLING HIDDEN AWAY.
MY NAME WAS NOW MOSES FRIEDLER.

WHAT ARE YOUR PLANS?
I'M GOING TO PALESTINE.
I WANNA GO TO AMERICA.
WHAT'S KEEPING YOU HERE?
MOST PEOPLE ARE GOING TO AMERICA. ANYWHERE BUT HERE!
YOU THINK? TO AMERICA?
OH, IF ONLY I COULD LEAVE THIS TERRIBLE COUNTRY AND GO TO AMERICA WITH YOU AT MY SIDE.
YOUR LOVING
LEAH
BUT YOU NEED A SPONSOR OVER THERE.
I'VE GOT AN UNCLE THERE.
YOU LUCKY DOG! CAN YOU SPEAK ENGLISH? I CAN HELP YOU WRITE A LETTER. FOR YOUR WATCH...
NOW ALL I COULD DO WAS WAIT. A FRIEND IN THE CAMP TOLD ME ABOUT THE JEWISH BOXING CHAMPIONSHIP THE U.S. MILITARY WAS HOLDING IN JANUARY 1946.
IT WAS FOOLISH, BUT I SIGNED UP UNDER MY REAL NAME.

I WANTED THE WHOLE WORLD TO KNOW THAT I WAS STILL ALIVE!

THE WINNER ON POINTS IS... HERTZKO HAFT!
I'M STILL HERE!!!!
I HEREBY AWARD HERTZKO HAFT THE TROPHY FOR THE BEST BOXER IN THE TOURNAMENT.
DO YOU SEE THESE NUMBERS, GENERAL? DO YOU KNOW ABOUT ALL THE BAD TIMES I'VE HAD TO GO THROUGH HERE IN GERMANY?
I WANT TO GO TO AMERICA.
WHERE'S YOUR FAMILY?
THEY'RE ALL DEAD. THERE'S NOTHING TO KEEP ME HERE ANYMORE.
IF YOU NEED ANY HELP, DROP BY MY OFFICE.

BUT GENERAL CLAY COULDN'T DO ANYTHING FOR ME, SO I HAD TO WAIT ANOTHER FOUR MONTHS UNTIL I BOARDED THE MARINE MARLIN IN BREMERHAVEN FOR NEW YORK.
I'M PROBABLY GOING TO STAY HERE, HERTZKO.
I'M SURE YOU'LL FOLLOW ON AT SOME POINT, PERETZ.
LOOK AFTER YOURSELF, HERTZKO!
WHAT ELSE CAN HAPPEN TO ME NOW...?

2

THE JOURNEY TOOK FOREVER, AND BECAUSE I DIDN'T HAVE ENOUGH MONEY, I HAD TO SLEEP ON DECK LIKE A LOT OF OTHERS.

WHAT'S WRONG? ARE YOU OK?
AH!!!
I SMELL BURNING! THE PEOPLE ARE BURNING!

AFTER A WEEK AT SEA, THE SHIP REACHED AMERICA.
WHAT KIND OF COUNTRY COULD IT BE THAT WAS LIT UP LIKE THAT?
I WAS 23 YEARS OLD. IT FELT LIKE ANYTHING WAS POSSIBLE NOW.

HERTZKO? WELCOME TO AMERICA!
UNCLE SAMUEL? IT'S NOT HERTZKO ANYMORE. IT'S HARRY FROM NOW ON!
WELL, FIRST YOU STAY WITH US FOR A WHILE.
Brooklyn
Coca Cola
THANKS, UNCLE!
IT'S NOTHING. WE'RE FAMILY, AREN'T WE?
YEAH... WHAT'S LEFT OF US...
DELI
RESTAURANT
I'LL INTRODUCE YOU TO HY ZIMMEL. HE'S A LAWYER. HE'LL SORT OUT YOUR PAPERS FOR YOU. YOU'VE REALLY CAUSED A BIG CONFUSION, HERR FRIEDLER!
KOSHER DELI

SO YOU'RE THE BOXING CHAMP!
ZIMMER
BOX!
I LOVE BOXING! IT'S A FANTASTIC SPORT! BROTHER, A CHAMP FROM EUROPE! I KNOW A COUPLE OF GUYS AT A PAPER. I'M SURE THEY'LL WRITE A PIECE ON YOU!
WELL, THAT MIGHT BE OVERSTATING IT...
IF YOU THINK...
NEWS
WILL YOU READ ME WHAT IT SAYS?!
"THE GERMAN HEAVYWEIGHT CHAMPION HAS ARRIVED... BEFORE WINNING THE HEAVYWEIGHT CHAMPIONSHIP IN MUNICH, HE WON 75 KNOCK-OUT FIGHTS IN GERMAN DEATH CAMPS." HMM, NOT BAD... EVEN IF I DON'T LIKE BOXING!
SOUNDS LIKE SOMEONE YOU SHOULD WATCH OUT FOR!
ARE YOU SURE? PLEASE LOOK AGAIN...
THERE'S NO WOMAN WITH THAT NAME LISTED HERE.
TRY OVER AT THE REGISTRATION OFFICE.
I'M SORRY, I CAN'T HELP YOU...
PABLANSKI... PABLANSKI... NO, NO ENTRY...
DON'T GET DOWNHEARTED. YOU CAME IN UNDER A FALSE NAME. MAYBE LEAH DID THE SAME.

KNOCK
YEAH?
I'M FRANK PALERMO.
I WANNA TALK BUSINESS WITH HARRY HAFT.
BUSINESS?
I'M A BOXING MANAGER. IS HE IN?
NO, HE'S TRAVELLING. I'M HIS UNCLE. CAN I HELP?
I WANT TO TALK TO HIM ABOUT THE BOXING BUSINESS HERE IN THE STATES. THERE'S A LOT OF MONEY TO BE MADE.
GIVE ME YOUR TELEPHONE NUMBER SO HE CAN CALL YOU.
YOU MAKE SURE HE CALLS ME.
YOU UNDERSTAND. CIAO!
HARRY!
WHAT?
WHAT DID HE WANT?
I'VE LIVED HERE TWENTY YEARS AND NOT ONCE HAVE I COME ACROSS A GANGSTER. BUT YOU'RE HERE FIVE MINUTES AND THERE'S ONE AT MY DOOR.
HE'S A BOXING MANAGER OR SOMETHING LIKE THAT. I SAID YOU WEREN'T INTERESTED. AND... YOU AREN'T REALLY INTERESTED, ARE YOU?

A BOXING MANAGER, YOU SAY? OY! WE HAVE TO GET A MOVE ON...
WHY?
YOU'RE GOING TO BE A BOXER! AND I'LL HELP YOU! LOOK, YOU JUST HAVE TO SIGN THIS.
Contract
WHAT WILL UNCLE SAM HAVE TO SAY ABOUT THIS?
DON'T YOU WORRY ABOUT THAT. I'M A MEMBER OF THE FAMILY. PLUS, YOU NEED WORK. WE'LL ALL EARN A LITTLE MONEY. TRUST ME!
WE'LL FIND YOU A MANAGER. YOU'LL SEE. SOON YOUR NAME WILL BE IN ALL THE PAPERS.
IF I BECAME FAMOUS, THEN EVERYONE WOULD READ ABOUT ME.
MAYBE...
...EVEN LEAH IF SHE WAS IN AMERICA.
AND IF SHE WAS SOMEWHERE ELSE, SHE'D READ MY NAME WHEN I BECAME WORLD CHAMPION.
THEN SHE'D KNOW I WAS LOOKING FOR HER!
UNCLE SAMUEL, I GOT A JOB!
GREAT! WHAT AS?
I'M GOING TO BOX PROFESSIONALLY!

SAM THREW YOU OUT?!
HE SAID HE'S GOT NO PROBLEM WITH ME PRIZEFIGHTING, BUT NOT UNDER HIS ROOF.
THAT OLD GUY!
LOOK, THIS HERE IS HARRY MANDELL. HE'S A BOXING MANAGER.
HI BUDDY!
WHAT ARE WE GONNA CALL HIM? WHAT'S HIS FIGHT NAME?
IT SHOULD BE IMMEDIATELY CLEAR THAT HE'S JEWISH. WHAT DO YOU THINK ABOUT...
HERSCHEL HAFT!
PERFECT! HARRY "HERSCHEL" HAFT. YEAH, IT'S GOT SOMETHING. IT STICKS WITH YOU.
MANDELL, GET THE GUY A CHEAP ROOM.
Movie
cine
AMERICA WAS GLEAMING AND BRIGHT, NOT LIKE THE DARK, GRIM EUROPE I HAD LEFT FAR BEHIND.

HOTEL
WONDER WHEEL
CYCLONE
ATLANtic
ARCA
Nathans
I WAS SURE THAT LEAH WAS HERE SOMEWHERE, PERHAPS EVEN NEAR HERE... IN NEW YORK?
Half Moon HOTEL
MANDELL TOOK ME TO CONEY ISLAND. THE HALF MOON HOTEL WAS A RUNDOWN FLOPHOUSE. MANDELL SAID THAT JEWISH GANGSTERS USED TO COME AND GO HERE.
JEWISH GANGSTERS?
SURE. THEY THREW ONE OF THEM FROM THE SIXTH FLOOR. NAME WAS KID TWIST.
HAHA! YOU AIN'T SUPERSTITIOUS ARE YOU, TOUGH GUY?
SOMEHOW IT EASED MY MIND KNOWING THAT THERE WAS SOMETHING LIKE JEWISH GANGSTERS HERE.

GRUNT!
GRUNT!
GRUNT!
GRUNT!
GRUNT!
Ruby's
FRESH
WAIT HERE... I'LL HAVE A WORD WITH WHITEY BIMSTEIN. HE'S THE BEST TRAINER THERE IS.
HEY, COME HERE!
LET'S TAKE A LOOK AT HOW YOUR BOY HANDLES HIMSELF IN THE RING...
...IF HE'S AS GOOD AS THEY SAY HE IS. GET UP THERE, FELLA!

TAKE iT EASY, BOYS!
Paff
HA, ROOKiE.
Paff
STOP! FOR GOD'S SAKE!

DIDN'T I SAY TAKE IT EASY?!!
AND?
HE'S TOO SLOW, NO GUARD, AND LOUSY TECHNIQUE.
NOW THE GOOD STUFF!
HE'S GOT A POWERFUL PUNCH AND CAN REALLY METE IT OUT.
WILL YOU TAKE HIM ON?
TAKE HIM OVER TO STILLMAN'S PLACE. WE'LL SEE HOW HE DEVELOPS.
HEY, YOU GOT A CONTRACT WITH THE KID?
YEAH.
I'LL GIVE YOU THIRTY GRAND FOR HIM.
HE AIN'T FOR SALE!

EVERLAST
YOUR ACCENT SOUNDS POLISH.
I'M FROM BEŁCHATOW. I WAS IN A CAMP.
OH, THEN YOU NEED SOMETHING VERY SPECIAL.

I HAD ALL THE GEAR I NEEDED MADE AVAILABLE TO ME AS A PROFESSIONAL BOXER.
AND THAT STAR FILLED ME WITH MORE PRIDE THAN ANY BRONZE TROPHY...

HE'S DROPPING HIS GUARD.
NOT SO STIFF, DAMMIT! HOW OFTEN HAVE I GOTTA SAY IT?!
Paff
AND? LEARNED ANYTHING, KID?
NOT STIFF MEANS JUST ME GETTING HIT!
IF YOU TAKE FIVE HITS JUST TO LAND ONE...
...YOU'LL DIE IN THE RING!

AFTER A MONTH, MANDELL FINALLY MANAGED TO ORGANIZE A COUPLE OF FIGHTS FOR ME.
WHO IS THAT GUY?
HE'S FROM EUROPE. HE FOUGHT IN A DEATH CAMP.
A REAL TOUGH GUY, HUH? WHAT'S HIS NAME?
IT SAYS HERE, "HERSCHEL" HAFT.
A JEW. BETTER WATCH OUT...
I BEAT BOTH LETTY AND CARDIONE WITH KNOCK-OUTS IN THE SECOND ROUND. AND I BEAT BILLY WEST ON POINTS IN THE SIXTH.
HERE'S YOUR SHARE, MINUS TRAVEL COSTS.
FORTY DOLLARS? MANDELL, I'M KILLING MYSELF HERE! AND MY NAME AIN'T EVEN IN THE PAPERS YET!
YOU'LL SEE. YOU'LL START GETTING BETTER FIGHTS. AND WHAT'S ALL THIS ABOUT THE PAPERS?
THAT'S THE MOST IMPORTANT THING! MY NAME'S GOTTA BE WRITTEN BIG IN THE PAPERS!

IT DIDN'T TAKE LONG BEFORE THE MONEY RAN OUT. AT SOME POINT, MANDELL STOPPED PAYING FOR THE TRAINING HALL AND I WAS OUT THE DOOR.
BUT I WASN'T GOING TO BE STOPPED SO EASY. NOT HERE IN AMERICA.
APOLLO
BOXING
125 th
BOXING
HARLEM.
I'D REACHED THE BOTTOM OF THE BOXING WORLD.
I'M SUPPOSED TO TRAIN HERE.
YOU'RE MANDELL'S KID? I WAS EXPECTING A BLACK GUY.
WHAT KIND OF ACCENT IS THAT YOU GOT?

POLISH AND GERMAN...
GET CHANGED AND LET'S GET STARTED.
HUH? A WHITE GUY IN HARLEM!
GET YOURSELF BACK DOWNTOWN!
I JUST IGNORED THEIR COMMENTS. THEY COULDN'T SCARE ME. NOT AFTER WHAT I HAD LIVED THROUGH IN EUROPE.
MATT MINCEY WEIGHS IN AT 205 POUNDS, 26 MORE THAN YOU. YOU WANNA TRY IT?
I'LL FINISH HIM IN TWO ROUNDS. AND YOU RECKON THAT THE FIGHT'S GOING TO BE ON TV?
YEAH, IT'S A BIG DEAL!
APOLLO
125th

SEPTEMBER 22, 1948.
JAMAICA ARENA, QUEENS.

I'VE GOT MONEY ON THE WHITE GUY!!
YEAH!

GONG!
WHAT ARE YOU WAITING FOR?!
THIS AIN'T A KINDER-GARTEN!
I WANNA STAY IN THE RING AS LONG AS POSSIBLE!
AND I WANNA SEE HIS BLACK ASS ON THE CANVAS, AND I MEAN NOW!

FROM THAT MOMENT ON, I WAS A KNOWN NAME. THE PAPERS AND TV CHANNELS REPORTED ON HARRY HAFT.
HARRY, THE PHONE FOR YOU!
ARE YOU HARRY HAFT, THE BOXER?
YEAH...

I READ ABOUT YOU IN THE PAPER. I'M FROM BEŁCHATOW. I KNEW YOUR FAMILY. I'M SORRY.
THANKS. IF YOU'RE FROM BEŁCHATOW, MAYBE YOU KNOW LEAH PABLANSKI OR SOMEONE FROM HER FAMILY?
YEAH.
DO YOU HAVE ANY IDEA WHERE SHE MIGHT BE?
I DON'T KNOW WHERE SHE IS NOW, BUT I KNOW SHE'S PROBABLY IN AMERICA.
NOW I WAS SURE THAT BEING FAMOUS WOULD LEAD ME TO LEAH.
FROM OCTOBER 1948 ON, I FOUGHT A SERIES OF FIGHTS. I WON SEVEN OF THEM.
BUT SOON MY LUCK RAN OUT.

LASTARZA IS NO SLUGGER. HE PUNCHES THEN STEPS BACK IMMEDIATELY.
STOP IT, MANDELL! I'LL BEAT HIM!
DON'T BE STUPID! WATCH OUT FOR HIS LEFT...
WHO IS HE ANYWAY...?
GONG!!!
STAY CLOSE!
...LEFT, RIGHT!
YEAH! THAT'S HOW YOU WIN POINTS!
PUNCH!
DAMMIT HARRY!!!
KEEP YOUR GUARD UP!!!
BUT IN THE FOURTH ROUND, LASTARZA SENT ME DOWN.
STAY DOWN!
YOU'VE GOT TIME TILL EIGHT...

GET YOUR ARMS UP!!!
YOU HEAR ME?! ARMS UP!!!
STOP!
WHAT ARE YOU DOING?!
WHY ARE YOU STOPPING THE FIGHT? HE CAN GO ON...
THE WINNER ON A TECHNICAL K.O....
ROLAND LASTARZA!
THIS IS BULLSHIT!!!
HOW OFTEN I GOTTA TELL YOU? ALWAYS KEEP YOUR FISTS UP!! YOU'VE BEEN IN THE COUNTRY LONG ENOUGH TO KNOW THE RULES OF BOXING HERE.
I THOUGHT I HAD TO BE UP AGAIN BY EIGHT!
SAVE THE LAME EXCUSES! YOU WERE THIS CLOSE...!

THAT WAS iT. MY CAREER WAS OVER. FiNISHED. AND ALL BECAUSE OF A STUPiD MiSTAKE.
Ring
MANDELL, WHAT DO YOU WANT?
GET BACK iN TRAiNiNG, PRONTO. I'VE GOT A FiGHT THAT'S GONNA GET US BACK iN BUSiNESS.
WHO?
ROCKY MARCiANO.
MARCiANO. NO ONE HAD BEEN ABLE TO BEAT HiM...
MY...
LAST... CHANCE!
WELL, LOOK AT THE POLACK WE GOT HERE!
Hi, CHARLEY. HOW YOU DOiNG?
WATCH WHAT YOU SAY TO HiM.
YOU KNOW HE'S ROCKY'S TRAiNER.
I HEARD YOU ESCAPED THE GERMANS. YOU KNOW WHAT? HiTLER WiPED OUT HALF MY FAMiLY iN WARSAW.
YOU WANNA SEE MY LUCKY NUMBERS?
THAT... THAT MEANS YOU SURViVED THE CAMPS?
44735

YOU GOTTA HELP ME, CHARLEY.
YOU KNOW WHAT I MEAN...
DON'T ASK ME TO DO THAT, HARRY! IF ROCKY'S PEOPLE FOUND OUT, I'D BE DEAD.
I'M HIS TRAINER!
AND I AIN'T GOT A CHANCE AGAINST ROCKY. AND I NEED THE FIGHT...
PLEASE... FOR EVERYTHING I HAD TO GO THROUGH...
FINE... I'LL BE HERE TODAY AND TOMORROW. I'LL SHOW YOU A FEW THINGS.
BUT NOT A WORD TO ANYONE. UNDERSTAND?!
IF I COULD WIN THE FIGHT, I'D BE IN THE BIG TIME AND MY NAME WOULD FINALLY BE SEEN EVERYWHERE.
I'D BE SO BIG THAT NO ONE COULD MISS ME. THEN LEAH WOULD FIND ME.
BUT ROCKY WAS A REAL TOUGH OPPONENT. NO ONE HAD BEATEN HIM!
YOU THINK YOU'VE GOT A CHANCE?
MIND YOUR OWN BUSINESS!
BECAUSE I'M GONNA BE NUMBER ONE!

GROSSINGERS
HOTEL
Tonight
ARTHUR
ELLEN
HYPNOTIST
YOU'LL SEE. IT'LL TAKE OUR MINDS OFF THINGS, HARRY.
HOTEL
GROSSINGERS HOTEL
WHATEVER YOU SAY...
YOUR EYES ARE GETTING HEAVY...
Tonight

THE GUY'S SUPPOSED TO BE SOME KIND OF PHENOMENON.
WHEN I RING THE BELL, YOU WILL STAND UP AND CRY, "LONG LIVE CAPTAIN SPALDING!"
Snap
A ROUND OF APPLAUSE FOR OUR GUEST!
CLAP
CLAP
CLAP
CLAP
Ding
LONG LIVE CAPTAIN SPALDING!
I CAN MAKE ANY ONE OF YOU DO WHAT I WISH... NO MATTER WHAT!
HA!
HA!
HA!
HMM...

THANK YOU, MR...?
MR. ELLEN, THAT WAS MIGHTY INTERESTING.
MANDELL, BOXING MANAGER. TELL ME, COULD HYPNOSIS HELP A BOXER WIN AN IMPORTANT FIGHT?
SURE, IF HE KNOWS HIS CRAFT.
I'VE GOT A BOXER HERE WITH A BIG FIGHT COMING UP, AGAINST AN UNBEATEN CHAMPION.
HYPNOSIS CAN HELP ANY ATHLETE ACHIEVE PEAK PERFORMANCE BY REMOVING THE BARRIERS THAT HAVE THUS FAR PREVENTED THEM FROM ACHIEVING IT SO FAR.
LISTEN, I'LL MAKE YOU A DEAL.
IF MY BOXER WINS, YOU'LL CASH IN ON THE PUBLICITY. WHAT DO YOU SAY?
SOUNDS GOOD. YOU KNOW, IF SOMETHING LIKE THAT GOT AROUND...
...I COULD OPEN MY OWN PRACTICE. IS IT REALLY A BIG FIGHT?
ALL THE NETWORKS WILL BE THERE.
AND THIS IS YOUR BOXER?
EVERYTHING HANGS ON THIS FIGHT. EVERYTHING I'VE WORKED FOR IS AT STAKE.

WHAT ARE YOU SCARED OF THE MOST?
WELL... MARCIANO PACKS A MEAN PUNCH.
WHAT ELSE?
THAT I'LL GET A CUT AND BLEED INTO MY EYE.
GOOD. WE'LL START THERE...
...YOUR EYES ARE GETTING HEAVY...
YOU ARE NOT AFRAID OF MARCIANO!
YOU WILL NOT FEEL HIS BLOWS, HARRY!
YOU ARE NOT SCARED...
YOU WILL NOT GET CUT!
I WILL NOW COUNT TO TEN AND YOU WILL WAKE UP.
YOU WILL NOT REMEMBER ANYTHING...
...UNTIL YOU HEAR THE FIGHT BELL.
Snap
YOU'RE READY.
I FEEL... REFRESHED...
I WAS GOING TO FIND LEAH. I'D NEVER BEEN SO CERTAIN.

ARENA
Tonight ROCKY MARCIANO vs. HARRY HAFT
R.I. AUDITORIUM
DON'T EMBARRASS US, HAFT!
...DON'T LET HIM GET CLOSE. HE'LL KILL YOU WITH INFIGHTING...
HEY! WHO LET YOU IN? ONLY THE BOXERS AND THEIR TEAMS ARE ALLOWED BACK HERE.

TAKE iT EASY. WE'RE iN CHARGE AROUND HERE. NOW GO GET SOME FRESH AiR.
ANYTHiNG YOU GOT TO SAY TO MY FiGHTER, YOU CAN SAY TO ME.
iF YOU SAY SO.
WE'RE HERE TO LOOK AFTER ROCKY.
AND I'M HERE TO LOOK AFTER HARRY HAFT.
THEN TELL HiM iT WiLL BE BETTER FOR HiM TO GO DOWN iN THE FiRST ROUND.
BEAT iT! YOU DON'T SCARE ME!
THEY TRiED TO FiNiSH ME OFF iN GERMANY AND I'M STiLL HERE!
LESS OF THE CHEEK. YOU EVER HEARD OF ViNCE FOSTER?
WE ADViSED ViNCE NOT TO BEAT TONY PELLONE iN MADiSON SQUARE.

VINCE WAS A TOUGH GUY, TOO...
AND NOW HE'S DEAD.
VINCE IS DEAD?!
DO WHAT YOU'RE TOLD AND YOU'LL LIVE TO READ ABOUT IT IN THE PAPERS TOMORROW.
WHAT WAS ALL THAT ABOUT VINCE? WHAT DO I DO NOW?
WHAT DO YOU WANT ME TO SAY?
YOU'RE MY MANAGER!
WE CALL THE POLICE.
AND HOW DO I PROTECT MYSELF BACK IN BROOKLYN?

NOT HERE
IN AMERICA.
NOT FOR
A BOXING
MATCH...

I'D NEVER BEEN SCARED OF AN OPPONENT.
BENLEE
BUT NOW I COULDN'T SHAKE THE FEAR.

I INSTINCTIVELY LOOKED FOR THE THUGS IN THE CROWD, BUT I COULDN'T SEE THEM ANYWHERE.
Gong
...I'M NOT SCARED...
BOTH FIGHTERS HAVE STARTED OFF CAUTIOUSLY.
HAFT, AN AGGRESSIVE FORWARD BOXER...
...LANDS THE FIRST CLEAN HIT, A HARD RIGHT TO MARCIANO'S BODY.

HAFT HAS TAKEN SOME HARD BLOWS, BUT NOW HE'S LANDING SOME OF HIS OWN HARD PUNCHES.
ROCKY FOLLOWS WITH TWO LEFTS TO THE HEAD...
...HIS OPPONENT LOOKS VERY GROGGY.
BARK

THERE GOES THE BELL.
IT'S GOING TO BE AN EXCITING ROUND TWO.

I AIN'T SCARED...

THE THIRD ROUND HAS STARTED HERE IN THE ARENA IN PROVIDENCE.
ROCKY OPENS WITH A LEFT AND A RIGHT TO HAFT'S HEAD...

HAFT MANAGES TO RECOVER, BUT MARCiANO FOLLOWS WiTH A LEFT HOOK TO THE BODY...
A SHORT CROSS...
BARK
THE REFEREE iS COUNTiNG...

THE FiGHT iS OVER.
THERE iS A GENEROUS APPLAUSE...
THE CROWD KNOWS FULL WELL THAT HAFT ENTERED A FiGHT HE COULD ONLY LOSE.

CLOSE THE DOOR!
WHAT HAPPENED, HARRY? YOU TOOK EVERYTHING HE GAVE YOU AND THEN YOU JUST GO DOWN?
YOU DON'T KNOW? DOES THE NAME VINCE FOSTER MEAN ANYTHING TO YOU?
WHAT ARE YOU TALKING ABOUT?
IF HE DOESN'T KNOW ANYTHING, THERE'S NO POINT TALKING TO HIM ABOUT IT.
I'M DONE. I'M THROWING IN THE TOWEL.
NOW, JUST CALM DOWN, HARRY. I'LL GET YOU A NEW FIGHT.

SAVE YOURSELF THE TROUBLE. I'VE HAD ENOUGH!
ARENA
Tonight
EXTRA! EXTRA! BOXING CHAMP FOSTER DIES IN CAR CRASH...

AT FACTORY
OOM CO.
BOXING!
PAT O'CO
ARENA
CHARLIE SALAS
VS.
LOUIS
NO

MIRIAM, HELLO?
ER... HELLO, IT'S ME, HARRY, YOUR NEIGHBOUR ACROSS THE STREET. I... ERM... I ALWAYS SEE YOU AT THE WINDOW.
REALLY? I'VE SEEN YOU, TOO.
DO YOU... MAYBE YOU WOULD LIKE TO GO OUT WITH ME TOMORROW?
HMM... I HAVE TO ASK MY MOTHER...
IT TOOK A LITTLE WHILE.
THAT DOESN'T MATTER.
HAVE YOU EVER BEEN TO A NIGHTCLUB?
NEVER! HAVE YOU?
THEN WHAT ARE WE WAITING FOR?

A PICTURE OF THE YOUNG COUPLE?
I SPENT MY LAST DOLLAR TAKING MIRIAM TO THE ICELAND SUPPER CLUB.
WHY NOT?
TUESDAY, TOO.
ON MONDAY, I PICKED HER UP FROM WORK ON FULTON STREET.
AND WEDNESDAY.
HAVE YOU THOUGHT ABOUT IT?
HRM... DO YOU WANT TO...

MIRIAM BECAME MY WIFE ON NOVEMBER 19, 1949.
AUNT SADIE AND UNCLE SAM, THANK YOU FOR COMING.
YOU KNOW THAT FAMILY HAS GOT TO STICK TOGETHER.
AND NOW YOU'VE FINALLY COME TO YOUR SENSES, YOUNG MAN! MAZELTOV!
AND MANDELL? YOU GOT A NEW FIGHTER ALREADY?
OH... YOU KNOW ME...

HOW DO YOU LIKE IT IN AMERICA, PERETZ?
RUSHKA AND I ARE STAYING! UNCLE SAM MIGHT HAVE A PLACE FOR US.
YOU CAN'T GET RID OF US THAT EASILY, HERTZKO!
AND YOU, BROTHER? HAVE YOU FINALLY SETTLED IN AMERICA NOW?
YES, PERETZ. MAYBE NOW I CAN FORGET WHAT HAPPENED...
LET'S DRINK TO THAT... TODAY, WE CELEBRATE!
LIKE WE DID BACK IN STRAUBING!

FOR RENT
CLEAN
Rutland Rd. 3
AFTER WORKING A FEW YEARS AS A STORE ASSISTANT...
...I OPENED A CORNER STORE IN BROOKLYN, JUST LIKE DAD HAD DREAMED OF DOING.

HEY, HARRY THE BOXER! WHAT YOU GOT ON SPECiAL TODAY?
FRESH APPLES FROM LONG ISLAND!
GiVE ME FOUR POUNDS. TELL ME AGAiN, WHAT WAS THAT iN THE THiRD ROUND?
HOW MANY TiMES HAVE I GOT TO TELL YOU?
I DON'T KNOW! THE FiGHT WAS RiGGED!
ROCKY NEVER CHEATED!
I HAD TO TAKE A DiVE BECAUSE THEY THREATENED ME.
THAT'S A DOLLAR!
THAT DAMN iDiOT! WHAT DOES HE KNOW?!
CLEAN
I WAS NOW A FAMiLY MAN WiTH THREE KiDS TO RAiSE. THE MEMORY OF LEAH SLOWLY FADED...
BUT iT NEVER DiSAPPEARED COMPLETELY.

...I DON'T KNOW! THE FIGHT WAS RIGGED!
ROCKY NEVER CHEATED!
I HAD TO TAKE A DIVE BECAUSE THEY THREATENED ME.
THAT'S A DOLLAR!
THAT DAMN IDIOT! WHAT DOES HE KNOW?!
I NEVER BELIEVED MY DAD'S VERSION OF THE FIGHT. BUT I WAS STILL PROUD TO BE THE SON OF SUCH A TOUGH GUY.
MY DAD WASN'T LIKE THE OTHER DADS IN BROOKLYN. I WAS OFTEN SCARED OF HIM. HE WAS HOT-TEMPERED, HE ONLY SPOKE BROKEN ENGLISH AND COULD BARELY READ AND WRITE.
GOD DAMMIT, ALAN. DON'T JUST SIT THERE. HELP ME WITH THE CRATES!
I WAS OFTEN ASHAMED OF HIM.
WE WERE POOR. DAD WORKED IN THE STORE EVERY DAY.
WHICH IS WHY WE WERE SURPRISED WHEN HE TOLD US IN SEPTEMBER 1963 THAT WE WERE GOING TO FLORIDA ON VACATION...
MIAMI

I WAS THIRTEEN. MY SISTER, HELENE, WAS NINE, AND MY BROTHER, MARTY, WAS FIVE.
WHERE'S THE POOL?!
THE BEACH ISN'T FAR!
MIRIAM, YOU TAKE THE KIDS TO THE POOL! ALAN, YOU STAY HERE.
LISTEN, I WANT YOU TO LOOK FOR SOMEONE IN THE PHONE BOOK. THE NAME'S LIEBERMAN. I WANT YOU TO CALL THEM.
THERE'S A WHOLE BUNCH OF PEOPLE WITH THAT NAME.
THEN CALL THEM IN ORDER AND ASK FOR LEAH PABLANSKI. AND NOT A WORD ABOUT THIS TO YOUR MOM!
HELLO...
DO YOU KNOW A LEAH PABLANSKI?
THEY HUNG UP...
DO YOU KNOW A LEAH PABLANSKI?
NO...?
I'M SORRY TO DISTURB YOU...
MICHAEL LIEBERMAN SPEAKING.
HELLO, CAN I SPEAK TO LEAH PABLANSKI?
WHO... WHO IS THIS? SHE DOESN'T WANT TO TALK.
MY NAME IS ALAN HAFT. PLEASE WAIT, THERE'S SOMEONE WHO'D LIKE TO SPEAK TO YOU.

DAD RENTED A CAR AND WE SET OFF FOR THE LIEBERMANS'.
MIAMI
WHO IS THIS WOMAN?
I KNOW HER FROM POLAND.
DID YOU TALK TO HER?
JUST TO HER... HUSBAND. HE SAID SHE DIDN'T WANT TO TALK TO ANYONE.
WHY?
DON'T HANG UP! I'VE COME ALL THE WAY FROM NEW YORK TO SEE HER.
PLEASE TELL HER THAT HERTZKO FROM BEŁCHATOW WOULD LIKE TO SEE HER...
HOW DO I KNOW?
NOW, NO MORE TALKING!
I DIDN'T KNOW WHAT I WAS DOING THERE. I WANTED TO BE AT THE POOL.

BUT TALKING BACK TO DAD WASN'T A GOOD iDEA.
I'M MiCHAEL LiEBERMAN. ARE YOU HERTZKO?
CALL ME HARRY... THiS iS MY SON, ALAN.
THiS iS OUR DAUGHTER, SARAH.
PLEASE TELL ME, HOW DiD YOU FiND US?

I GOT A CALL FROM THE SOCIETY FOR SURVIVORS OF BEŁCHATOW. THEY TOLD ME THAT LEAH WAS LIVING IN MIAMI UNDER A NEW FAMILY NAME.
YOU WON'T BELIEVE EVERYTHING I'VE DONE TRYING TO FIND HER.
WHEN I TOLD LEAH THAT YOU HAD CALLED, SHE SAID SHE JUST HAD TO SEE YOU.
LEAH HAS WITHDRAWN FROM LIFE. NOT EVEN FRIENDS AND FAMILY CAN VISIT HER ANYMORE.
SHE'S ASHAMED. SHE WAS SUCH A BEAUTIFUL WOMAN...
LEAH'S GOT CANCER...
SHE'S UPSTAIRS.
I'LL HELP HER DOWN.

TO ME, DAD WAS THE TOUGHEST GUY IN THE WORLD. I'D NEVER SEEN HIM CRY BEFORE.
HERTZKO...
TELL ME, HERTZKO...
...DOES MY SARAH LOOK LIKE ME?
YEAH, SHE DOES...
MICHAEL, I WOULD LIKE TO SHOW HERTZKO OUR GARDEN AND BE ALONE WITH HIM A WHILE.
THAT'S A GOOD IDEA.

WOULD YOU LIKE SOMETHING ELSE TO DRINK, ALAN?
GOODBYE, ALAN. TAKE CARE OF YOUR FATHER.

IKH HOB DIKH KEYNMOL NIT FARGESN.*
WE CAN GO.
LAST NIGHT SHE TOLD ME EVERYTHING. SHE WAS SO HAPPY TO FIND OUT THAT YOU HAD SURVIVED.
YES.

*YIDDISH: "I NEVER FORGOT YOU."

NO MUSIC!

IT'S GOOD YOU CAME TODAY.
ONE DAY, I'LL TELL YOU EVERYTHING.
IT TOOK ANOTHER FORTY YEARS UNTIL MY FATHER FINALLY TOLD ME HIS LIFE STORY.

Photo: Alan Haft's Private Archive

Harry "Herschel" Haft as a professional boxer, 1948/49

Boxing in concentration camps

A report by Martin Krauss

The fate of the man who as Hertzko Haft only survived Auschwitz because he boxed there for the SS, and who fought under the name of Harry Haft in the late 1940s against the best heavyweight boxers of his day, is unique. However, the terrible experiences he endured under National Socialism were by no means an isolated case – a whole host of boxers were interned at Nazi concentration camps. Most of them were murdered there.

For life and death

During the first half of the 1940s, large numbers of boxers from all across Europe were imprisoned and abused at Nazi concentration camps. Many of them were forced to take part in show fights for the amusement of the SS men. Sport, or this perverted form of sport, actually took place in almost every concentration camp run by the Germans. Football matches were held and the camp at Terezín also had its own league system. Handball competitions were organized and Auschwitz even boasted a high bar for gymnasts.

The awareness of sports activities at the camps was suppressed for a long time. Veronika Springmann, a historian from Berlin, has spent years researching the subject of 'Sport in concentration camps' and has referred to a wealth of reports that have never been properly evaluated by historians. Springmann sees the motivation for organized sports in concentration camps in the needs of the arms industry for manpower. This would explain why certain groups of prisoners were kept physically fit. "From 1942, the Nazi leadership came to view the concentration camps also as a business enterprise."

Boxing, however, assumed a special place here. As a rule, boxers fought for life and death – it was a singularly sadistic spectacle. World class professionals, such as the former world flyweight champion Young Perez and the boxing champion Leone Efrati, were forced into the ring to fight in front of bellowing SS soldiers. Outstanding amateurs like the Greek friends Salamo Arouch and Jacko Razon were involved, as well as top boxers like Rukelie Trollmann and Kid Francis. There were Olympic athletes, such as Heinz Levy and Imre Mándi, as well as men who had never boxed before like Noach Klinger and also Hertzko Haft.

For decades, these men were forgotten about, almost as though they had never existed. Journalists and historians have now started compiling information about some of the boxers, while only fragmentary data exists today about the lives of others.

In many cases, not even the most rudimentary facts have survived, as the Freiburg-based historian Diethelm Blecking found when visiting the Neuengamme Concentration Camp Memorial near Hamburg: "Boxers who won Olympic medals and national championships are supposed to have been in Neuengamme, including a black heavyweight from France whose name remains unknown."

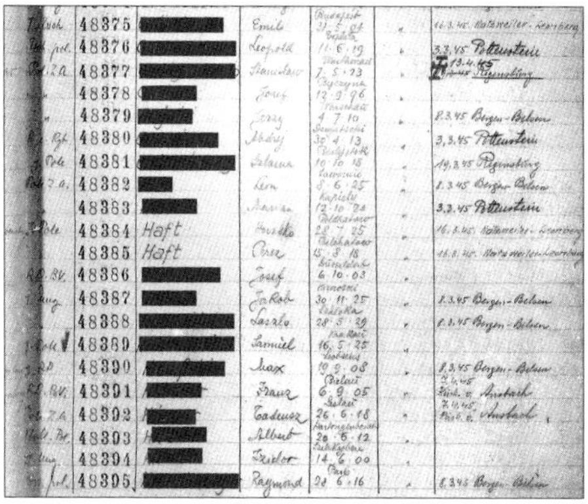

48375	[redacted]
48376	[redacted]
48377	[redacted]
48378	[redacted]
48379	[redacted]
48380	[redacted]
48381	[redacted]
48382	[redacted]
48383	[redacted]
48384	Haft
48385	Haft
48386	[redacted]
48387	[redacted]
48388	[redacted]
48389	[redacted]
48390	[redacted]
48391	[redacted]
48392	[redacted]
48393	[redacted]
48394	[redacted]
48395	[redacted]

Photo: Archive of Flossenbürg Concentration Camp Memorial

The names of Hertzko and Peretz Haft in one of the prisoner registers at Flossenbürg concentration camp.

Hertzko Haft's ordeal

Quite a lot is known about Hertzko Haft, who later went by the name of Harry Haft in the US, and who also appeared using the first names of Herschel and Hertzka. In 2006 and at the age of 78, some six decades after his experiences in German camps, he revealed his story to his son, who documented the events of his father's life for all to read. Although some details, on closer inspection, are historically incorrect or at least dubious, the conclusion drawn by the publisher Bernd M. Beyer hits the nail on the head: "This changes nothing about the truthfulness and forcefulness of his experience." The story of Hertzko/Harry Haft happened largely in the way it is depicted in Alan Scott Haft's book *Harry Haft: Auschwitz Survivor, Challenger of Rocky Marciano*, and in the present graphic novel by Reinhard Kleist. It is an incredible, yet believable, biography.

Hertzko Haft was born on 28 July 1925 in Bełchatow, Poland, a medium-sized industrial town near Łódź. His parents were Moische and Hynda Haft. His father traded in fruit, which he brought into the town from surrounding farms. When the Second World War started on 1 September 1939, with Germany's attack on Poland, Bełchatow was one of the first targets. The town was bombed by the German Air Force and captured a few weeks later on 5 October. The local Jewish community was held in a ghetto, where they were subjected to forced labour. In 1941, Hertzko Haft was arrested and taken to labour camps in Poznań and Strzelin. On 2 September 1943, he was deported via the Bochnia detention camp to Auschwitz-Birkenau.

Hertzko Haft had the prisoner number 144738 tattooed onto his forearm. However, neither his name nor that of the other approx. 3,000 prisoners who arrived on that day from Bochnia was recorded in the concentration camp's registers. This is not the only example that shows how overwhelmed the camp's bureaucratic apparatus must have been as a result of the mass murder plans.

Haft was later moved to the labour camp at Jaworzno, 20 kilometers from Katowice, where the prisoners had to work in coal pits. This is where Hertzko Haft boxed while being protected by an SS man whose name is unknown, but who is referred to as "Schneider" in the book and graphic novel.

When the Red Army advanced ever closer during the course of the Second World War, the prisoners, including Hertzko Haft and his brother Peretz, with whom he was reunited in Jaworzno, were sent on death marches towards the west. The first march began on 17 January 1945, and led them to Gross-Rosen in Lower Silesia, about 50 kilometers from Wrocław. The Gross-Rosen concentration camp was evacuated shortly afterwards and, after yet another death march, the prisoners were back at the Flossenbürg camp in Bavaria. The arrival of the Haft brothers was recorded there on 13 February 1945. As is noted in Haft's own recollections, reports of cannibalism began to emerge from Flossenbürg and other concentration camps, where the final year of the war began with catastrophic hygiene conditions, acute overcrowding and dramatic food shortages. The Haft brothers were taken from Flossenbürg to Leonberg near Stuttgart on 16 March 1945, which is also documented by the camp's bureaucracy. When they were once more sent out on a death march, this time from Leonberg to the Kaufering and Mühldorf subcamps in Bavaria, Hertzko Haft managed to escape. His brother Peretz, however, reached the destination camp and was liberated shortly afterwards by the US Army.

Hertzko Haft vs. Rocky Marciano

At the end of the war, Hertzko Haft initially remained in Bavaria, where he won a boxing competition for Jewish 'Displaced Persons' in 1946 in front of a crowd of 10,000. Shortly afterwards, Haft emigrated to the US and started a new life with a

Photo: Alan Haft's private archive

Hertzko Haft (shirtless, centre of picture) at the awards ceremony of the Jewish Boxing Championship in Germany in 1946.

career as a professional boxer in 1948. His boxing career got off to a highly promising start with ten wins in a row, most of which were knock-outs. This was followed by a series of defeats, and on 18 July 1949, Haft was knocked out in the third round of his last ever fight in Rhode Island Auditorium in Providence by the man who would go on to become the heavyweight champion of the world, Rocky Marciano. It cannot be said with any certainty if this fight really was fixed by organized criminal elements, as Haft claimed during his life. While it was true that Marciano received protection from the mafia, he was also without doubt one of the best heavyweight boxers of the last century, and can be compared to the likes of Joe Louis and Muhammad Ali. Haft's record after 21 professional fights read: 13 victories, including 8 knock-outs, and 8 defeats, 5 of which were by knock-out.

Photo: Alan Haft's private archive

After his boxing career: Hertzko Haft and his future wife Miriam Wofsoniker on their first date in October 1949.

US boxing and the mafia

The International Boxing Club (IBC) was founded in 1949 in New York to promote boxing matches. The promoters involved hoped to establish a monopoly on the top fights, particularly those held at New York's Madison Square Garden. This was made even more significant by the fact that the professional boxing business faced interesting new challenges with the advent of television. The IBC was able to boast close contacts to the most appealing boxers of the time, such as the long-standing world champion Joe Louis and the new star of the heavyweight scene, Rocky Marciano. The aim of monopolizing the market was quickly achieved, and the IBC controlled 47 of 51 championship fights in the US between 1949 and 1955. The monopoly was secured by close connections to the US mafia, who didn't just make money from the takings and the TV rights, but also controlled the fighters and earned more cash by betting on fixed fights. Key figures of influence on professional boxing were Frankie Carbo and Frank "Blinky" Palermo. After Rocky Marciano announced his retirement, the mafia succeeded in managing Sonny Liston, who also went on to become a heavyweight champion of the world.

"My father was illiterate and could only manage to read the funnies and the results columns in the sports section of the newspaper," reports Alan Scott Haft on the difficulty of working on his father's confession. This was why Harry Haft was never able to turn to historical works and documentation to compare them to his own memories. He tried to suppress his dramatic experiences for almost sixty years. His son describes him as a "brutal and violent man"; this lasted a very long time before he understood "all the bad things that he had been through in his life". Harry Haft was still alive to witness the publication of the American edition of his biography. He died in Florida on 3 November 2007.

Forgotten champions

Hertzko/Harry Haft's life story is unique, yet it is also partly exemplary for other, comparable biographies. We will now take a closer look at some more people's lives.

Victor "Young" Perez was born in 1911 in French Tunisia as Victor Younki and grew up in a Sephardic family in the Jewish quarter of Tunis. At the age of 14, Perez became a boxer and left in 1927 as a professional for France, where he had a relationship for a while with the future actress Mireille Balin. In 1931, he beat the American fighter Frankie Genaro and became the world flyweight champion. "The return to Tunisia was a triumphal procession," wrote the historian Diethelm Blecking. "100,000 ecstatic supporters filled the Avenue Jules-Ferry and saluted the champion." In November 1938, exactly on 9 November – the Night of Broken Glass – Perez travelled to Berlin for a boxing match. Due to his fear of what he saw when he arrived there, he only left his hotel room for the fight. He lost his bout at the Deutschlandhalle against the Austrian Ernst Weiss – and was dismissed with a storm of hatred from the spectators.

When the German Armed Forces occupied Paris, Perez attempted to flee but was denounced before he could leave. He was arrested on 21 September 1943 and shortly afterwards deported to Auschwitz, where he ended up as a slave labourer for the chemicals company IG Farben at Auschwitz-Monowitz (also known as Auschwitz III). He was also forced to box there for the amusement of the SS. Diethelm Blecking writes of one of the fights: "The spectators consisted of 200 SS men who had come from many different places, even from neighbouring camps. There were a further 100 to 150 barrack leaders and kapos from the camp hierarchy, as well as hundreds of prisoners who looked on from 100 meters away." As the Allied troops moved closer, the SS sent the Monowitz prisoners on a death march to Gliwice shortly before the end of the war. Young Perez failed to survive the march and was killed on 22 January

1945, probably after being shot by one of the guards.

In 1943, the 17-year-old Strasbourg Jew **Noach Klieger** was deported to Auschwitz. The camp commander was Heinrich Schwarz, who had reportedly set up a boxing club for his private amusement. Klieger had never boxed before, but he joined the club when they were looking for volunteers. "I don't know what suddenly made me raise my hand at the time," Klieger later told the journalist Helmut Kuhn. As one of the prisoners who took part in show fights every Sunday on behalf of the SS henchmen, Klieger received an additional bowl of soup every day. In total, he appeared in 22 fights – "and I didn't win any of them". He claimed that he fought together in Auschwitz with two European boxing champions and a previous professional footballer whose names are unknown. He was later transferred to the Dora-Mittelbau concentration camp in Thuringia and, as the Red Army approached, sent out on death marches. Klieger managed to survive. After 1945, he became one of the commanders on the legendary 'Exodus' ship that carried Jews to Palestine. He later found work in Israel as a journalist and became chairman of Maccabi Tel Aviv, which is still one of the best basketball clubs in the world. He never boxed again.

Leendert "Leen" Josua Sanders from the Netherlands made his professional debut as a middleweight at the age of just 18. In 1929, he succeeded in beating the German Gustav Eder but failed to win any major titles, despite such victories against strong opponents. His greatest achievements were winning the Dutch lightweight and middleweight championships. In 1936, he lost a European championship bout to Felix Wouters from Belgium and appeared in a professional fight in Amsterdam as late as December 1940. In 1941, the Jewish Sanders family was deported to Auschwitz. Sanders' wife, his sons, his parents, and seven siblings were murdered there. Leen Sanders survived for the sole reason of having boxed at the camp. After the liberation, Sanders returned to the Netherlands and fought in two more professional bouts. Leen Sanders died in 1992 in Rotterdam at the age of 83.

Leendert Sanders

The Italian **Leone "Lelletto" Efrati** began his professional career in 1935 as a 20-year-old. A featherweight fighter, he went to the US three years later and by the end of 1938 managed to land an important bout. He went ten rounds with the American world champion Leo Rodak before losing. The fight was probably not licensed as a title fight and there are rumors that Efrati, who was listed as number ten in the world for his category, could have stayed in the US if he had beaten Rodak. As things turned out, he was sent back to Italy.

Efrati was deported to Auschwitz around 1940. The Italian journalists Alessandro Ferrarini and Paolo Consiglio have carried out some research on Efrati's life story:

"In Auschwitz, he was forced to take part in cruel boxing matches in which he fought against much bigger opponents – all for the entertainment of the guards." According to Ferrarini and Consiglio's findings, Efrati survived all that. "However, when his brother was seriously abused by the guards, he sought revenge. Nobody ever defeated him – except the armed German soldiers: Leone Efrati was killed in Auschwitz on 19 April 1944."

Salamo Arouch from Greece appeared in his first boxing match at the tender age of 14 and became the welterweight champion of the Balkans while still only 17. Arouch's entire family was deported to Auschwitz after the German Army occupied Greece. His childhood friend and fellow boxer Jacko Razon, a Jew like Arouch, was also taken away with his family. Arouch would soon have to box several times a week in front of the SS soldiers. He claimed to have fought in a total of 208 bouts – without losing any of them, even though he regularly had to fight heavier opponents. "They were just like cockfights," Arouch later told the *New York Times*. The defeated fighters were mostly killed. "Salamo Arouch survived," writes Diethelm Blecking, "thanks to his boxing skills and thanks to the winnings that his ability guaranteed to those who bet on him." Shortly before the end of the war, Arouch was deported to Bergen-Belsen where he was finally liberated. Arouch went to Palestine, got involved in building the nation of Israel and embarked in 1955 on a career as a professional boxer. This career didn't last long, however, and the only fight he lost was a knock-out. He then founded his own transport company. Arouch's story was filmed as *Triumph of the Spirit* in 1989 by the American director Robert M. Young, with Willem Dafoe in the main role. During the final credits, Dafoe and Arouch can be seen dancing together in a moving scene in a Greek taverna.

Salamo Arouch

The middleweight boxer **Jacko Razon** became the Greek amateur champion in 1939 at the age of 18. He learned how to box together with his childhood friend Salamo Arouch. What's more, Razon played in goal for Olympiakos Saloniki, his hometown soccer club, in the Greek first division. When the Germans conquered Greece in 1943, Razon was deported to Auschwitz. In Auschwitz-Monowitz, he was commissioned by the camp commander Heinrich Schwarz to set up a boxing club: twelve boxers, Jews and non-Jews, professionals and amateurs. The former world champion Victor "Young" Perez was among them, and Noach Klieger from France was probably also involved. Jacko Razon had to box at least once a week, often against heavier opponents. He managed to win most of the more than 120 fights that he took part in. It is said of him that he used his good contacts to the camp's kitchen, where he received his extra rations, to help many other prisoners. He was later transferred to Gliwice, and then on to Mittelbau Dora where he also boxed. In Bergen-Belsen, the last station of his ordeal, he was supposed to fight against his old friend Salamo Arouch. The liberation of the camp in May 1945 by the British Army prevented this fight from ever taking place. After 1945, he organized what was described by the British Mandate authorities as an illegal emigration of Holocaust survivors to Palestine. When the fate of his friend Salamo Arouch was filmed in 1989 as *Triumph of the Spirit*, Razon filed a complaint, claiming that it was his own life that was being depicted. His protests fell on deaf ears, however.

At the end of the 1920s, the German Sinto **Johann "Rukelie" Trollmann** from Hanover was one of the best amateur boxers in northern Germany. He turned professional after not being sent to the 1928 Olympic Games, presumably because he was regarded as a gypsy. On 9 June 1933, he fought Adolf Witt from Kiel for the German light-heavyweight crown. This title was unoccupied because the actual champion, the Jewish boxer Erich Seelig, had had to emigrate. Trollmann fought the better fight but the nazified boxing association refused to award him the victory. The spectators and a tearful Trollmann protested until he was crowned champion, although the title was taken away from him just four days later. The association argued that a German boxer must "not weep in public". Trollmann continued boxing at fairgrounds and was regularly threatened with reprisals. In 1938, he was arrested. He was initially sent to a labour camp and then forced to join the German Army on the Eastern Front. In 1942, he was transferred to Neuengamme concentration camp, where he was forced to box for the entertainment of the SS men. When he grew too weak to continue fighting, he was shot on 9 April 1943.

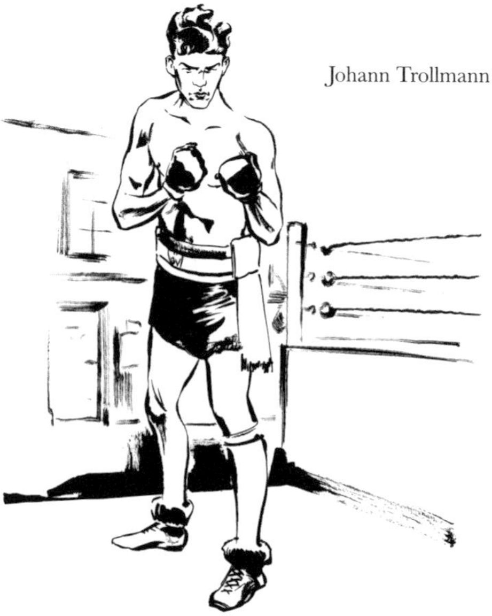

Johann Trollmann

Although **Tadeusz "Teddy" Pietrzykowski** from Poland first learned how to box at the comparatively late age of 20, he quickly became Warsaw's and Poland's bantamweight vice-champion. After the Germans invaded Poland in 1939, Pietrzykowski signed up to the defence of Warsaw. When Poland capitulated in the spring of 1940, he attempted to make his way to France, but was arrested and deported to Auschwitz. It is thought that he took part in 40 to 60 boxing matches at Auschwitz-Monowitz. It is reported that he also fought against the Dutch middleweight boxer Leen Sanders. Pietrzykowski was later transferred to Neuengamme, where he fought in another 20 or so bouts. After yet another transfer to Bergen-Belsen, Pietrzykowski was finally liberated in April 1945 by British soldiers.After the war, Pietrzykowski organized sports training in the Polish Army. The Polish writer Józef Hen based his work *The Boxer and Death* on the events of Pietrzykowski's life, and the story was filmed in 1962 by the Czechoslovakian director Peter Solan and featured the East German actor Manfred Krug.

The Italian Jew **Francesco Buonagurio** established himself as a boxer in France using the name **"Kid Francis"**. He became the French bantamweight champion in 1925 and a year later he lost the fight for the European championship narrowly on points to Henri Scillie. On one occasion in 1931, Kid Francis took part in a show fight at the legendary Madison Square Garden in New York against Fidel LaBarba. Francis amazed the 8,000 spectators present with a "frenzied boxing performance", as the *New York Times* wrote at the time. When the German Army occupied Paris, Kid Francis was arrested and shortly afterwards deported to Auschwitz, where the SS forced him to take part in show fights. In 1943, Francesco Buonagurio was murdered in the concentration camp.

The majority of the men who fought for their lives in concentration camps also met their death there. The few who succeeded in fighting their way through to survival were scarcely able to report the suffering they had endured. They were seriously traumatized and very little attention was paid to their fate. Historians and sports journalists are only gradually beginning to cover this complex and important topic.

Sport in the DP camps

When the Second World War came to an end in 1945 and the surviving prisoners from the concentration camps were liberated, some 7 million displaced persons were living in the 4 occupied zones. Sport was played at all the DP camps, which were temporary facilities for the accommodation of homeless people. The most popular sports were football and boxing. The journalist Eric Friedler reports a boxing tournament at which Hertzko Haft also appeared: "One of the highlights of the sporting activities in the DP camps came at the end of December [1946] when a three-day boxing tournament was held at the Circus Krone in Munich. 120 Jewish boxers of all weight categories fought in front of crowds of over 10,000 people, who had travelled from all the occupied zones." Regarding the question as to why boxing proved to be so popular, Friedler writes that it represented "for many people an image of the rekindled Jewish strength and therefore became a symbol for a future life in dignity and freedom".

Martin Krauss
lives and works as a freelance sports journalist in Berlin. He regularly contributes to the newspapers *Jüdische Allgemeine, the tageszeitung (taz)* and *Jungle World*. Books include: *Schmeling. Die Karriere eines Jahrhundertdeutschen* (Göttingen 2000) and *Kampftage. Die Geschichte des deutschen Berufsboxens* (with Knud Kohr, Göttingen 2000).

STILLMANS
GYM
TRAINING
HERE DAILY

Reinhard Kleist was born near Cologne in 1970. After studying Graphic Design at Münster University of Applied Sciences, he settled in Berlin in 1996. There he works in a studio which he shares with the comic book artists Naomi Fearn, Fil, and Mawil.

In 1994, while still at university, Reinhard Kleist published the elaborately designed graphic novel *Lovecraft*, for which he was awarded the most important comic book award in Germany, the Max und Moritz Prize at the International Comic-Salon, Erlangen, in 1996. He subsequently made the departure to more conventional graphic novels long before the rise of their popularity in Germany, with the publication of *Amerika* in 1998. This is an extensively personal narrative told in harsh black and white. His graphic novel on the life of the country musician Johnny Cash saw Kleist achieve his international breakthrough in 2006. *Johnny Cash, I See a Darkness* has been translated into twelve languages and repeatedly awarded prizes, including the Sondermann at the Frankfurt Book Fair in 2007 and the Max und Moritz Prize (2008). In 2008, Reinhard Kleist travelled through Cuba for four weeks. His impressions and experiences were captured in the gripping book *Havanna. Eine kubanische Reise.* More importantly, however, his time in the socialist island state was preparation for his second big graphic novel biography, *Castro* (2010), in which he captures on paper the life story of the former revolutionary leader Fidel Castro through a half a century of Cuban history. *The Boxer* was previously printed in installments in the *Frankfurter Allgemeinen Zeitung* from March to September 2011.

As well as a graphic novel author, Reinhard Kleist is also a professional illustrator. In 2010, he designed, among other things, a prize-winning issue of the *Süddeutsche Zeitung Magazins* on the theme of genocide.

Alan Scott Haft, born in 1950, is the eldest son of Hertzko (Harry) Haft. After studying at the University of Miami Law School, he now lives with his family in Albuquerque in New Mexico, where he is a professional lawyer. In 2002, he wrote his father's life story, which appeared under the title *Harry Haft: Auschwitz Survivor, Challenger of Rocky Marciano.*

Thanks:

Alan Haft
Andreas Platthaus
Martin Krauss
Nebojsa Tabacki
Anne Marie Kau
Erika Kleist
Lothar Kleist
Susanne Hellweg
Joachim Werth
Ralf Liebe
Flix
Julia Treptow
Boris Kiselicki
K77
Naomi Fearn, Fil, Mawil
Michael Groenewald
Paul, Mina und Claudia Jerusalem-Groenewald

Everyone at Carlsen Verlag